Unicorn

Unicorn
A mythological investigation
Author: Robert Brown Jr.

Original title: *The Unicorn* (1881)
Cover image: *A Virgin with a Unicorn* (c. 1604–05), Domenico Zampieri (1581 – 1641)
Lay-out: www.burokd.nl

ISBN 978-94-92355-07-2

VAMzzz Publishing
P.O. Box 3340
1001 AC Amsterdam
The Netherlands
www.vamzzz.com
contactvamzzz@gmail.com

UNICORN
A mythological investigation

Robert Brown Jr.

VAMzzz PUBLISHING

contents

Post Scriptum

'Cry to the moon to sink her lingering horn
In the dim seas, and let the day be born.'

Foreword

THIS LITTLE brochure is a contribution, however humble, to the science of psychology; not merely a notice of curious, still less of idle, fancies. The study of man to be successful must commence with his earlier, that is to say, simpler, phases. The 'solar myth,' vaguely so called, is often ridiculed but never by anyone who has carefully examined it; and the history of the Lion and the Unicorn exhibits one aspect of the ideas of Time and Kosmic Order as shown in the most obvious divisions of period—Day and Night. The indirect influence of our present civilization and the repetition of phenomena produce a sadly deadening effect upon the vast majority of minds as regards appreciation of the external world, and render it extremely difficult for us to place ourselves near the mental standpoint of primitive, or even of archaic, man. We do not wonder at the sun, or at the genius which has contrived by the use of only ten signs to express any number, or indeed at anything which, though marvellous in itself, is somewhat familiar to the senses and ordinary apprehension. Even scientific research often resolves itself into an anatomical dissection, which is equivalent to the knowledge of the way about a cathedral, combined with an appreciation of the principles of masonry, but accompanied by total ignorance of, or utter indifference to, the real forces which produced the building.

With respect to the evidence adduced in the particular case, its *combined* weight is specially to be considered; the various points are not links in a chain, the failure in any one of which is fatal, but items in a description.

As, according to Prof. Ludwig Noiré, the discovery of the axe assured the triumph of the kingdom of man upon earth, so the idea of Time, solar (day), lunar (week-month), and sidereal (year), was a mighty mental axe with which Thought hewed its way to noble victories. I treat here merely of the Day and of that which by division makes it—the Night, and of but one mythic phase of these; yet, be it remembered, the idea of Day contained the germ of the idea of Eternity, so far as such a concept is possible to man; for Time is Division, a Day the primary division, and Eternity merely infinitely reduplicated Time.

BARTON-UPON-HUMBER, Oct. 1, 1881

I
The heraldic Unicorn

THE SCIENCE of Heraldry has faithfully preserved to modern times various phases of some of those remarkable legends, which, based upon a study of natural phenomena, exhibit the process whereby the greater part of mythology has come into existence. There we find the solar Gryphon, [1] the solar Phoenix, [2] 'a demi-eagle displayed issuing from flames of fire,' [3] the solar Lion, and the lunar Unicorn, which two latter noble creatures now harmoniously support the Royal Arms. I propose in the following pages to examine the myth of the Unicorn, the wild, white, fierce, chaste Moon, whose two horns, unlike those of mortal creatures, are indissolubly twisted into one; the creature that endlessly fights with the Lion to gain the crown (κορυφή) or summit of heaven which neither may retain, and whose brilliant horn drives away the darkness and evil of the night, even as we find in the myth that 'venym is defended by the horn of an Vnicorne.' [4] As the Moon rules the sea and water, [5] so the horn of the Unicorn is said to purify the streams and pools, and we are told that other animals will not drink until this purification is made; for the Unicorn ere he slakes his thirst, like the sinking Moon, dips his horn in water. As the Moon, Artemis-Selenê, is the 'queen and huntress, chaste and fair,' so is 'the maiden Unicorne' [6] 'in the Classical and Middle Ages the emblem of chastity.' [7] 'Their inviolable attachment to virginity, has occasioned them to become the guardian hieroglyphic of that virtue.' [8] According to Upton, quoted by Dallaway, the Unicorn 'capitur cum arte mirabili. Puella virgo in sylva proponitur solaque relinquitur, qui adveniens depolita omni ferocitate casti corporis pudicitiam in virgine veneratur, caputque suum in sinu puellae imponit, sicque soperatus deprehenditur a venatoribus et occiditur, vel in regali palatio ad spectandum exhibetur.'

Dallaway conjectures that 'the tester or armour for horses' heads in the centre of which a long spike was fixed, suggested the idea of a beast so defended by nature.' With respect to this view it may suffice to remark that the Unicorn is found on the archaic Cylinder-seals of Babylonia and Assyria, [9] as well as on the Horn of Ulf, [10] whereas 'the *Chanfron* with a spike projecting from it was adopted in 1467; probably this is the earliest date.' [11] The Testiere is first mentioned in the time of Edward I., and '*Chanfron* or *Champfreins*, pieces of steel or leather to cover the horse's face,' [12] came into vogue about the end of the thirteenth century. *Chanfrous* is an obsolete north-country term meaning very fierce. [13]

The Lion is the only animal that appears on the shields in *The Roll of Arms known as the Roll of King Henry III.*; the Unicorn, however, although not found on any shield in *The Roll of Karlaverok*, is mentioned by the herald who composed the MS. *Siege de Karlaverok*, now in the British Museum. He says:—

> '*Robert le seignour de Cliffort,*
> *A ki raisons donne confort*
> *De ses enemis emcombrer,*
> *Toutes les foiz ki remembrer*

Ki puet de son noble lignage.
Escoce pregn à teismoignage,
Ke ben e noblement commence,
Cum cil ki est de la semence
Le Conte Mareschal le noble
Ki par dela Constentinoble
A l'unicorn se combati
E desouz li mort le abati.

Robert the lord of Clifford,
To whom reason gives consolation
To overcome his enemies,
Every time he calls to memory
The fame of his noble lineage.
He calls Scotland to bear witness,
That he begins well and nobly,
As one who is of the race
Of the noble Earl Marshall,
Who beyond Constantinople
Fought with the Unicorn
And struck him dead beneath him.' [14]

The Gryphon, it may be observed, appears in the Roll as a Charge:—

'Symon de Montagu,
Ke avoit baniere e escu
De inde, au grifoun rampant de or fin.

Simon de Montagu,
Who had a banner and shield
Blue, with a griffin rampant *of fine gold.*' [15]

Sir Harris Nicholas observes that 'the exploit which is said
to have been performed by the Earl Marshall at Constantinople in
slaying a unicorn, which probably referred to a tradition familiar

at the time of some deed of one of the Marshall family in the Holy Land,' is not 'elsewhere commemorated.' [16]

In opposition to the opinion that the Unicorn could be captured by means of the stratagem above mentioned, it was more generally held that, like the Gryphon, [17] 'the Unicorne is never taken alive; and the reason being demanded, it is answered, that the greatnesse of his mind is such, that he choseth rather to die than to be taken alive.' [18] The real reason why both Gryphon and Unicorn are safe from capture is sufficiently obvious.

Cnut is said amongst other 'naval devices,' to have 'exhibited unicorns, centaurs, dragons, lions, dolphins, and human figures. The swift unicorn, either Anglo-Saxon or Dane, was obliged to fly before the two Norman leopards [or perhaps "lions" [19]]. Hence the naturalization of the emblematical unicorn in Scotland, and its return into England under the Stuart dynasty.' [20]

'The earliest extant example of the unicorn as a supporter in the royal arms of Scotland, appears to be that which occurs in the royal achievement carved above the gateway of Rothsay Castle. The Lyon king of arms, who examined it carefully last summer, told me that this carving appeared to him to be contemporaneous with the part of the building in which it is inserted, which, considering the style of the architecture and various entries in the Exchequer Rolls relative to the building of Rothsay Castle, he was disposed to assign to the time of Robert II. or III. [1380-1400]. In 1486 or 1487 two gold coins were struck, value respectively 18s. and 9s., and called the unicorn and half-unicorn, from the circumstance that they bore on one side the figure of a unicorn sejant supporting the royal escutcheon. In the same reign—that of James lll.—we first find unicorn pursuivant.' [21]

The following instances (amongst many) exhibit the Unicorn as a Charge:—

- The Arms of Sir John Rest, Lord Mayor of London in 1516, are Azure, on a Fess, between 3 Crosses Milroine, Or, a Unicorn couchant, Gules. This position of the Unicorn is very unusual. Mythologically, the bronze-red setting Moon. The Family of Harling bore Argent, a Unicorn Sejant, Sable; mythologically, the Moon in eclipse.
- The Family of Musterton bore Gules, a Unicorn with dexter leg raised, *i.e.*, tripping, Argent; mythologically, 'the Moon walking in brightness.' [22]
- The Family of Farrington bore Sable, 3 Unicorns, Current, Argent, 1 & 1 & 1; mythologically, the wild white Moon of triple aspect, [23] flying through the dark clouds.
- The Family of Shelley bore Gules, 3 Unicorn's heads couped, by 2 & 1.

The Tincture of the Unicorn is generally Argent, *i.e.*, the ordinary colour of the Moon, Leukotheê, 'the White-goddess,' [24] the Semitic Lebhânâ, the Pale-shiner, as distinguished from the burning, golden Tammuz-Adonis, the Akkadian Dumuzi or 'Only-son' of the diurnal heaven.' [25] 'The proper colour of the moon we in Heraldry take to be Argent, both for the weakness of the light, and also for the distinction betwixt the blazoning of it and the Sun; and therefore when we blazon by Planets, we name Gold *Sol*, and Silver *Luna*.' [26]

One or two Crests in which the Unicorn appears are of special interest inasmuch as most archaic ideas seem to have been unconsciously preserved in them. Thus:—

- The Crest of the Bickerstaff Family is the Sun with sable rays (*i.e.*, the nocturnal sun), surmounted by a Unicorn rampant, *i.e.*, the nightly triumph of the Moon over the Sun. In a variant form of this device the Unicorn is statant.
- The Crest of the Curteis Family is a Unicorn passant, between four trees; mythologically, a most interesting allusion to the archaic myth of the Grove of the Underworld. [27]

The Heraldic Moon is either Increscent, *i.e.*, the new moon with horns turned towards the dexter side of the shield; in Complement, *i.e.*, the full moon; Decrescent, *i.e.*, the waning moon with horns turned towards the sinister side of the shield; or in Detriment, *i.e.*, when eclipsed. [28] In this state it is emblazoned Sable. The Face in the Orb [29] is shown at times.

James I. introduced the (Scottish) Unicorn, argent, as the Sinister Supporter of the Royal Arms; and Guillim describes the Arms of Charles I. as 'supported by a *Lyon* rampand, SOL: and an *Unicorn*, LUNA.' [30]

Footnotes

1 Vide R. B. Jr., *G.D.M.* i. 334 *et seq.*; ii. 58-9. 'A male Griffin is distinguished by two straight horns rising from the forehead, and rays of gold which issue from various parts of the body' (Cussans, *H.H.* 93), the horned and radiate Sun (vide *G.D.M.* cap. IX. sec. iii. *Taurokerôs*).

2 Vide R. B. Jr., *The Archaic Solar-Cult of Egypt*, in the *Theological Review*, Oct. 1878, p. 525.

3 Cussans, *H.H.* 95.

4 *The Boke of Saint Albans*, xliii.

5 Vide sec. VIII.

6 Spencer, *An Elegie for Astrophell*.

7 Fosbroke, *E.A.* ii. 1022.

8 Dallaway, *Inquiries into the Origin and Progress of the Science of Heraldry in England*, 1793, p. 421.

9 Vide sec. III.

10 Vide Frontispiece. And sec. VI.

11 Fosbroke, *E.A.* ii. 892.

12 *Ibid.* 878-9.

13 Halliwell, *Dict. of Archaic and Provincial Words*, in voc.

14 Wright, *The Roll of Caerlaveroek*, 11-12.

15 Wright, *The Roll of Caerlaverock*, 17.

16 *The Siege of Carlaverock*, 186.

17 'The Griffon having attained his full growth, will never be taken alive' (Guillim, *D.H.* 259).

18 *Ibid.* 176.

19 Vide Scott, *Lord of the Isles*, vi. 35. Also Cussans, *H.H.* 79, upon the *quaestio vexata* whether the Shield of England originally bore Lions or Leopards.

20 Brunet, *Regal Armorie of Great Britain*, 219.

21 Letter from Thomas Dickson Esq., dated July 1, 1880.

22 *Job*, xxxi. 26.

23 Vide sec. VI.

24 Vide sec. VIII.

25 Vide R. B. Jr., *G.D.M.* i. 256.

26 Guillim, *D.H.* 111.

27 Vide sec. XII., subsec. 3.

28 Vide sec. V.

29 Vide secs. V., VII.

30 *D.H.* 440. The Throne is thus represented as firmly established as the course of nature.

ll
Opinions respecting the terrestrial existence of the Unicorn

AS THE UNICORN was not found in the flesh near home, and as its terrestrial existence was firmly believed in, it became necessary to locate the animal in some distant region. Perhaps the most celebrated of his supposed haunts is the English Version of the Old Testament, where the word 'unicorn,' in deference to the Μονοκέρως of the LXX., the Unicornis of the Vulgate, has unfortunately been introduced in several passages. The animal really referred to is the Rêm, the Assyrian Rimu or Wild Bull, respecting which the Rev. W. Houghton observes:—

'The species of wild cattle hunted by the Assyrian monarchs is either the *Bos primigenius* or some closely allied species; it is apparently identical with the gigantic *urus*, which Caesar and the Roman legions saw in the forests of Belgium and Germany.' [1]

Thus we read;—'He hath as it were the towering horns (lit. eminences) of a wild bull.' [2]

And again;—'Glorious is the firstling of his bullock, and his horns (*i.e.*, two horns) are like the horns of a wild bull.' [3] Here the LXX. absurdly read κέρατα μονοκέρωτος τὰ κέρατα αὐτοῦ, and our translators render the singular by the plural to preserve consistency. The other passages in the Old Testament where the Unicorn is mentioned are similar.

The cuneiform ideograph for the Rêm is ⬡ or ⬡ each of which forms show the two projecting horns in front.

Compare our letter A, originally the Phoenician and Moabite Stone ⬡, *i.e.*, the rude representation of a bull's horns.

So the form ⬡ (*i.e.*, ⬡ doubled) is the plural, 'cattle,' which, when domesticated, appear ⬡ , *i.e.*, in an enclosure ⬡ .

Pliny observes that the Unicorn 'cannot be taken alive;' [4] and Guillim remarks that 'some have made doubt whether there be any such beast as this or not. But the great esteem of his Home (in many places to be seen) may take away that needlesse scruple.' [5] Horns, no doubt, can be seen in various places, and the spiral tusk of the Narwhal was accustomed to be sold as the real horn of the unicorn; and as an accredited part of that animal, forming [a supposed] direct proof of its existence, it used to fetch a very high price.' [6] 'The heirs of the Chancellor to Christian Frisius of Denmark valued one at 8,000 imperials. In an inventory of the sixteenth century, we have, 'Item, two unicorns' bones, garnessyed with gold.' 'An unicorn horn at Somerset House, valued at 500*l*., occurs in the Inventory of the Plate of King Charles I.' [7] 'When the whale fishery was established, the real owner of the horn was discovered, and *the unicorn left still enveloped in mystery*. The name Monodon ["One-tooth"] is not strictly correct, as the Narwhal possesses *two* of these tusks, one on each side of its head.' [8] These twisted ivory tusks made excellent unicorns' horns.

The next animal in this competition is the Oryx (a name used by Aristotle, who probably refers to the Indian Nylghau), supposed by some to be the Unicorn of the Old Testament, and having long straight horns, which when seen in profile exactly cover each other, and so give a unicornic appearance. 'There is in the Museum at Bristol a stuffed antelope from Caffraria, presented in 1828. It is of the shape and size of a horse, with two straight taper horns, so nearly united, that in profile it shows only a single horn.'[9] The Oryx, however, is no Unicorn.

Next, as to the Rhinoceros. Pausanias describes the African species, 'Aithiopian Bulls, which they call "Nose-horn" (Ρινόκερως), because each has a horn at the end of its nose, and another small one above it'—the Rhinoceros 'gemino cornu' of Martial— 'but on its head there are no horns.'[10] The Keitloa, a kind of black Rhinoceros, is two-horned; as are the Muchocho and Kobaoba, the two white kinds. The Indian Rhinoceros, however, is one horned; but 'the so-called "horn" is not a true horn, being nothing but a process of the skin, and composed of a vast assemblage of hairs.'[11] The 'Indian Ass' of Aristotle, which he describes as having but one horn, is probably the one-horned Rhinoceros, the horn of which, like that supposed to belong to the Unicorn proper, has always been highly valued, and regarded as a detectant of poison. But no kind of Rhinoceros at all resembles the various representations of the Unicorn, is an opponent of the Lion, or answers generally to the mythical character of the mysterious creature.

Aldrovandus, amongst his other monsters and curiosities, speaks of a unicornic animal called the Camphurch, which apparently not being one of the fittest, has not survived. Apropos of the *lusus naturae*, it may be remembered that Plutarch mentions how 'a ram's head with only one horn' was brought to Perikles from one of his farms, which occasioned a prophecy that he would attain to supreme power in the state. [12] Here we trench on the symbolical, and so are reminded of Daniel's goat with 'a notable horn between his eyes,' [13] namely that Alexander, who, strange to say, adopting the horns of Ammon, reappears in the *Korân* [14] as Dhoulkarnain, 'the Two-horned.'

Having noticed the various actually existing animals that have been named in this connexion, it only remains to add that the Unicorn has been prudently relegated to those remote regions which are, or rather were, the special abodes of many wondrous creatures. Amongst these favoured localities was the great Hercynian Forest, in which, according to a report repeated by Caesar:—

'Est bos [a vague term applied to any large and strange animal] cervi figura, cujus a media fronte inter aures unum cornu existit, excelsius majisque directum his, *quae nobis nota sunt*, cornibus.' [15]

The vague description of Pliny, [16] seems to point to a kind of Rhinoceros. Cardan, following Pliny 'with advantages,' describes the Unicorn as rare, with the hair of a weasel, the head of a deer, the body of a horse, thin legs and inane, and one horn three cubits in length. [17]

Garcias has preserved a very interesting incident, namely, that the Unicorn 'was endowed with a wonderful horn, which it would sometimes turn to the left and right, at others raise, and then again depress.' [18] The progress of the lunar horn, of course, here supplies the basis of the myth. Oppian, Aelian, and many others refer either to the Unicorn itself, or to unicornic creatures.

Hesychios defines the Monokerôs vaguely as θηρίον φοβερόν; [19] Souidas prudently, as 'an animal which has by nature one horn.' [20]

Footnotes

1   Gleanings from the *Natural Hist. of the Ancients*, 172-3.

2   Numbers, xxiii. 22.

3   *Deuteronomy*, xxxiii. 17.

4   *Hist. Nat.* viii. 21; vide sec. I.

5   *D.H.* 175.

6   Rev. J. G. Wood, *Illustrated Natural History*, 85-6.

7   Fosbroke, *E.A.* i. 393.

8   Rev. J. G. Wood, *Illustrated Natural History*, 86.

9   Brunet, *Regal Armorie of Great Britain*, 218.

10   Paus. IX., xxi. 2.

11   Rev. J. G. Wood, *Illustrated Natural History*, 153.

12   *Perikles*, vii.

13   *Daniel*, viii. 5.

14   *Sura*, xviii.

15   *De Bello Gallico*, vi. 20.

16   *Hist. Nat.* viii. 21.

17   Vide the Monoceros, Unicornu, Einhorn, etc., described in Jonston, *Historia Naturalis*, 1657.

18   Apud *Penny Cyclopædia*, in voc. *Unicorn*.

19   In voc. *Monokeratos*.

20   In voc. *Monokerôs*.

The Unicorn in Archaic art

A UNICORNIC animal frequently appears in archaic art, but whilst asserting that all non-natural animal-figures or partly human figures when used in a religious connexion are symbolical, I do not for a moment contend that all unicornic animal-figures represent the moon; but merely that the creature whose form is familiar to us in heraldry, a kind of horse-stag or antelope, is a lunar emblem. Thus on a Babylonian Cylinder [1] representing Bel encountering Tiamat, who, whatever else she may represent, is the Dragon of Chaos, the monster who rises on her hind legs, has a beak, crest, wings and a single horn; and is altogether very similar to one of the Seven Wicked Spirits that make war against the Moon-god Sin, as the representative of kosmic order. [2] This latter creature, a reduplication of the drakontic Tiamat, rises similarly on its hind legs, and has a crest, wings, and single horn. [3] Tiamat herself is elsewhere represented as two-horned. [4] The horn has various meanings in symbolism, [5] the majority of which are not of a lunar character. But the following examples of the Unicorn, its allies, and opponents, are, in my opinion, certainly more or less connected with lunar symbolism;—

I.

On an Assyrian sardonyx Seal in the Louvre Museum, [6] is represented a crowned personage, behind whom is a serpent erect on its tail; his right hand grasps a dagger, and his left the horn of a Unicorn-goat, standing on its hind legs with the fore legs bent and head turned from him, the mouth touching the conventional Tree; above the animal, the crescent moon. The King (?) is about to slay the Unicorn, beneath the fore legs of which is a lozenge. With this design must be considered;—

II.

Another Babylonian Gem figured by Lajard, [7] on which is shown the king in the same attitude, grasping by the head a crowned and apparently human-headed and winged goat, in the same attitude as the Unicorn-goat. Beneath the fore legs of the crowned goat is a representation, apparently the yoni, the equivalent of the lozenge; and above the creature the crescent moon and behind it the conventional Tree, on the other side of which is a Goat in the same attitude as the crowned anima] except that its head is regardant [8] towards the Tree, as in No. I. The goat's two horns are close together so as to form but one, and beneath its fore legs is a figure composed of two crescent moons addorsed and fastened together. All the animals are salient. With both these designs let us consider;—

III.

An Assyrian Cylinder [9] of great interest, said to portray 'Merodach, or Bel, armed for the conflict with the Dragon;' but which I prefer to call 'The Sun-god and the Moon-god arranging the preservation of Kosmic Order.' On each side of the representation is a palm-tree;

in front of the one on the right hand Merodach ('the Brilliance-of-the-Sun') stands fully armed, on a leopard-like animal, [10] and above his crowned head is the solar star, the key to the symbolism. Merodach's right hand is raised as if in oath on a treaty, as is the right hand of a human figure in another long garment, in front of and apparently conversing with him. Behind this second figure are two Unicorn-goats, counter-salient, with heads regardant as in the last example. Above the Unicorns and the second figure, which I believe represents the Moon-god, is a crescent moon, curiously divided into three parts, [11] by what seem to be handles. Beyond the Unicorns is a second Palm-tree. The unarmed Moon commissions the warrior Sun to go forth to the great contest.

In all three instances we find the Unicorn, the Crescent-moon, and the Tree. [12] In the first two representations the Unicorn is being attacked and overcome by a personage whose crown and attire are very similar to those of Merodach. The type is evidently a familiar one; the Unicorn's horn in each case almost touches the Tree, to which its head always turns. In No. II. the Man-goat strives with the Man; the Goat, the reduplication of the former, does not: there is sometimes peace between the Unicorn and its assailant, and sometimes war. In No. III. the Leopard, which, as it could be trained to hunt, was a fit type of the Hunter-sun, is at peace with the Unicorns; whilst Sun and Moon consult together against darkness and chaos. The remarkable position of the two Unicorns indicates, I think, the monthly cycling progress of the moon, 'there and back' (counter-salient). Reduplication is a noted feature in symbolism; and we have here (1) the Moon-god, (2) the crescent moon, (3) the young moon, and (4) the old moon.

The next type to be noticed in this connexion consists of a divine personage between two other symbolical beings, whose hands or arms he grasps in a friendly manner;—

IV.

Divine four-winged personage, with round cap on head, and long fringed robe reaching to the ankles, but leaving the right leg exposed as ready for action as in the case of Merodach. [13] His right hand grasps the wrist of an androkephalik winged animal rampant, with human hands but lion's feet; his left hand grasps the right fore foot of a winged Unicorn, rampant, with hoofs. [14]

V.

Variant phase. [15] A similar personage, but without wings, stands in the same attitude between two semi-human, Dagonic (semi-piscine) figures, one of which has a large eye, the other has apparently its cap drawn down over the eye. To the right is the winged circle (not solar), the familiar type of the head of the Assyrian Pantheon. [16]

VI.

Third variant phase. [17] A similar personage between two androkephalik, winged, rampant animals. To the right the Moon-god in his crescent boat above the Sacred Tree. [18] The helmet of the creature next the Moon-god is horned.

In this representation I think we have the Demiurge Bel, whose eldest son in the formal Pantheon is Sin, the Moon-god, making a covenant between the Sun and Moon for the preservation of kosmic order. [19] The second creature in No. VI. is a reduplication of the Moon-god, whose introduction in his crescent [20] gives the key to the symbolism, whilst preserving the secret of it. The Moon-god, as 'Lord of growth,' [21] is stationed immediately over the Tree of Life. Both Sun and Moon are sea divinities as in No. V. [22] If this interpretation be correct we have the lunar Unicorn (No. V.) as the equivalent of the lunar fish and the lunar androkephalik animal.

VII.
On a Phoenician gem found at Cnidos [23] is represented the sun radiate, a large crescent moon, and between the two a small circle—perhaps the planet Venus, whilst below are two rude heads of a unicorn bull and cow. [24]

VIII.
A Unicorn-bull stands near the Sacred Tree, on the other side of which is a priest with a knife. [25]

IX.
The well-known bas-relief at Persepolis called 'Lion devouring a Bull,' is in reality 'Lion attacking a Unicorn.' The latter animal, semi-rampant and regardant, and with only one large horn, is seized behind by the lion. On this group Professor Rawlinson remarks;—

'This is a representation of a lion seizing and devouring a bull;

the latter animal is evidently powerless to offer any resistance to the fierce beast *which has sprung upon him from behind.* [26] In his agony the bull rears up his fore-parts, and turns his head feebly towards his assailant. . . . This favourite group, which the Persian sculptors *repeated without the slightest change from generation to generation.*' [27] The design was favourite because highly archaic and symbolical. No man has ever seen a lion attack a unicorn, but the contest between sun and moon, between day and night, was watched from the first with the closest interest. Sun and moon may equally combine against darkness and chaos, or contend against each other.' [28]

X.
A Persian Cylinder [29] shows the Unicorn-goat held in the arms of a divinity; [30] opposite is the sun radiate.

XI.
Another Assyrian scene from Layard [31] shows a man adoring a winged Unicorn-bull, above which appear the sun radiate, the crescent moon, and also the seven planets. It will be remembered that the Unicorn-stag is the creature which I regard as especially lunar; the representation shows how familiar is the idea of a Unicorn.

XII.
'Tree of Life, between two Gryphons.' [32] This cylinder-scene represents the Sacred Tree [33] between two winged Unicorns (not Gryphons) rampant, each turned towards it. The Tree is of the archaic

palm-type. With this may be compared the two Unicorns and the Palm in No. III.

XIII.

'Cow [34] and calf before a tree; over them the Sun and Planets. The representation of the animal presents a striking analogy to that of the bull *regardant* on the coins of Sybaris. Conical seal.' [35] The seal in question shows the Unicorn-cow (or bull) with the usual *prominent* (lunar) *eye*, before the tree; and, as frequently, regardant. [36] The horned moon it will of course be remembered, is frequently connected with the bull or cow, indeed more frequently than with the Unicorn; and the Bull and Cow, emblems of increase, are also connected with Night as a period of growth. The nocturnal Sun, too, is at times bovine; in contradistinction to the diurnal and leonine Sun. [37] We must expect to find frequently a mixture of ideas in a symbolical representation. This Unicorn-cow (if a cow it be) seems, as shown by the calf, to be kosmogonic as well as lunar; but the old attitude of the head, the prominent eye, the single horn and the tree are still preserved. 'The maiden unicorn' can have no calf; but the Old Moon is at times seen in the Young Moon's arms, [38] *i.e.*, when in addition to the sun-lit portion of the moon, the obscure portion is faintly visible on account of the reflection of the 'earth-shine;' called *lumen incinerosum*, a Cinderella-moon.

XIV.

It is convenient to notice next the archaic coinage of Sybaris referred to by Mr. King. Sybaris was colonised from Achaia, B.C. 721, and the coins in question may be placed prior to B.C. 600. Leake describes the type as 'Bull standing to left, with head reverted;' and remarks, 'This type is probably symbolical of the river Crathis.' [39] As in previous instances no attention is paid to the circumstance that the animal, whatever else it may be, is a unicorn, in this case a unicorn-bull. I do not absolutely assert that it is a lunar emblem; but it is certainly a link in the chain of unicornic representations, and has faithfully preserved the regardant attitude. As one of a series it is quite unconnected with the river Crathis, a circumstance also shown by the fact that this class of symbolical river-representations were not unicornic but purely bovine with respect to the head, such as that of the Acheloös, one of whose *horns* was broken off in his contest with Heraklês. [40]

XV.

The demi-Unicorn-bull alone, and also the heads of the Lion and Unicorn-bull fronting each other, as if combatant, appear on coins of Kypros. Archaic coins of Sardis also show the Demi-lion and Demi-bull (not Unicorn-bull), the same type, combatant. On another coin of Sardis the demi-Unicorn-bull appears alone. [41]

XVI.

Another Sardian coin shows the heads of the Lion and Unicorn-bull addorsed and joined at the neck, a fore foot of each being added. This type, is almost certainly borrowed from Persia; at Persepolis the double Unicorn-bull-capital appears, the bodies of the bulls being joined below the neck, and a fore foot of each being added. [42] This is probably ornamentation as distinct from symbolism.

XVII.

Unicornic monsters are also shown on Persian gems, cylinders, and sculptures. These creatures, however, are not lunar, but reproductions of the Akkadian and Assyrian evil-spirits, Tiamat and her brood, who often attack the Moon-god. 'One of them has the griffin head, a feathered crest and neck, a bird's wings, a scorpion's tail, [43] and legs terminating in the claws of an eagle.' [44]

XVIII.

A very interesting Assyrian or Babylonian Cylinder given by Creuzer [45] from Ker Porter and Guigniaut, shows above in the centre the Supreme Divinity, having the crescent moon and seven planets on his right hand, and the eight-rayed radiate sun on his left. Beneath the crescent stands the Moon-god armed, 'auf ein ungeflügeltes Einhorn [Unicorn] tretend.' [46] Before him stands the figure of a votary, behind whom and beneath the Divinity is the Sacred Tree, beyond which and beneath the sun is the figure of the Sun-god armed, and holding over the Tree what is apparently a necklet. A cuneiform inscription accompanies. Here, again, we have a scene of kosmic harmony; Divinity, Sun-god, and Moon-god, sun, moon, and planets, and the Tree of Life, which, being placed under the Divinity, is apparently a symbol of him in his effects. The direct connexion between the Crescent-moon and the Unicorn appears very strikingly. The Moon-god stands upon the Unicorn exactly in the same way as in other instances [47] he stands upon his crescent.

XIX.

The Assyrian sculptures show many representations of unicornic animals, *e.g.*:—

    1. Assurnatsirpal hunting Wild Bulls (about B.C. 884), North West Palace, Nimrud. Two bulls are represented, each with a single large horn.

    2. Assyrian Oxen (Koyunjik). [48]

    3. The Ibex or Gazelle. [49]

    4. The familiar representation of a small Fallow-deer, carried by a branch-bearing divinity.

This treatment is apparently partly conventional, but I do not think with Sir G. Wilkinson [50] that the sculptors represented under the form of the Unicorn-bull the Rhinoceros of which they had only heard, since widely different animals are so portrayed. Some representations show the two horns of the Ibex.

XX.

A Cylinder, 'found on the site of Nineveh,' [51] shows above the emblem of divinity, sun, crescent-moon, and seven planets, as in No. XVIII. Below, a man on horseback is apparently pursuing a Unicorn-antelope, in attitude almost rampant and regardant. Beyond this, another Unicorn, also regardant, is standing suckling a young kid. A human figure, apparently a priest, stands before a trident and another emblem. The combination is evidently symbolical, but its signification is obscure. The regardant attitude of the Unicorns is very noticeable.

XXI.

Amongst miscellaneous Assyrian unicornic representations may be noticed;—

1. A most heraldic pair of Unicorns' heads on a clay tablet. [52]
2. The head of a Unicorn-bull at the end of a chariot-pole, on which are also carved two winged Unicorn-bulls respectant. [53]
3. A Unicorn-ibex above a lotus-flower, from the royal cylinder of Sennacherib.

XXII.

D'Hancarville [54] and Taylor the Editor of Calmet's *Dictionary of the Bible*, [55] give the following unicornic coin-types, said to be Mardian;— [56]

1. A coin from Hunter's collection. A composite animal with one horn, a bull's body and legs, wings, and human head, upon which the *modius* (corn-measure), a usual adjunct of Serapis, whose cult was introduced into Egypt from Sinope. [47] Rev. The Triquetra. Here for the first time we meet with this purely lunar emblem, *i.e.*, three crescent moons issuing from the full moon, in connexion with the Unicorn.
2. Two Unicorn-bulls or Bull and Cow addorsed, after the type of the Persepolis capitals; above, the Triquetra. Rev. The Triquetra.
3. Unicorn-bull sinking down as if dying; above, a circle. The victory of sun over moon, or the waning moon (?). Rev. The Triquetra; variant phase as three legs. [58]

XXIII.

Lion pulling down a Unicorn-bull. [59] Calcedony. Of this example Mr.
King remarks, 'The technique of this intaglio is altogether Assyrian, and the subject justifies the conclusion that it is of Phoenician
workmanship.'

XXIV.

'The conjoined fore-quarters of two Winged [Unicorn-] Bulls.' [60] Mr.
King adds, 'Probably to be understood as an astrological talisman,
allusive to the Sign Taurus. Sard scarabeus.' The zodiacal Taurus,
however, is not unicornic, and the type is the same as that of the
Persepolitan capitals, which are certainly not zodiacal. It is singular
how rarely those who reproduce these representations have noticed
their unicornic character.

XXV.

The coins of Samos show a very interesting type;—A lion's scalp,
lion's head, or lion's head with open mouth. Rev. (of the first type)
Demi-unicorn-bull. At Samôs was a shrine of Dionysos Kechenôs, [61]
'the Gaper,' a solar divinity like the Apollôn Kechenôs of Elis; [62] the
open-mouthed Lion being a type of the raging, devouring Sun, Athamas. [63] The coin-type thus represented Day and Night, the Lion and
the Unicorn, or the Sun and Moon.

XXVI.

The Unicorn-bull, in one instance regardant, appears also upon some
Kretan coins. 'The circumstance of a single horn [as shown on var-

ious coins] perplexed the learned medallist Pelerin, who remarked it, without being able to offer any explanation of it.' [64] Kretan coins show various Semitic types, *e.g.*, 'l'arbre cosmique, identique à l'arbre de vie.' [65]

XXVII.

On the cup of Kourion [66] in Kypros are shown, amongst other devices, two unicorn-goats, each standing on one side of some conventional object, and with one fore foot resting upon it. The twisted horn in each case is near the Tree, whose type is well reproduced at the present time by the trees in toy Noah's arks.

XXVIII.

The Unicorn also occurs in 'early [Egyptian] paintings;' but, according to Sir G. Wilkinson, 'the Egyptian unicorn, even in the early time of the twelfth dynasty, was the rhinoceros.' [67] Yet at the same time we find a Unicorn-antelope depicted, [68] the animal couchant, the horn long and straight, and the tail standing straight up in an unnatural manner, in exactly the same way as the tail of the Kamic Gryphon is represented, [69] an additional circumstance in illustration of the fact that the representation is symbolical. The sound of the Unicorn-ideograph is given as '*St.*, Typhon,' and that of the Gryphon as '*Baru*, Baal; *Set*, Typhon.' Now 'Set ou Soutekh personnifie l'ardeur et la force redoutable du soleil'—Gryphon; but as the 'meurtrier d'Osiris, il est le dieu du mal et personnifie les ténèbres,' [70] and may thus be connected with the nocturnal unicorn. Sir G. Wilkinson observes, 'Many animals are introduced in the sculptures, . . . some of which are purely the offspring of *disordered imagination*; and the winged quadrupeds, sphinxes, or lions, with the head of a. hawk or of a snake, and some others equally fanciful and unnatural, *can only be compared to the creations of heraldry.*' [71] A 'disordered imagination' should be the last thing appealed to in explanation of such creations; in the abstract the same explanation might be given of the forms of the gods; and it is much more probable to suppose that some reason, symbolical or otherwise, underlies the efforts of the artist.

XXIX.

The discoveries of Schliemann at Mykênê have revealed, as might be expected, several instances of the Unicorn, although the author does not notice any of them in this aspect. Thus on a gem [72] is shown the familiar Unicorn-cow or Ox, in duplicate, as usual regardant, and each with a calf; but, as has sometimes been remarked on similar representations, no udder is shown. [73] The design is evidently symbolical, though it is by no means improbable that by the time it got as far west as Mykênê the original meaning was forgotten or unknown. But we have already met on Assyrian ground [74] with the peculiar type of two Unicorns standing opposite each other with reverted heads, and the circumstance is a link between the art of Mykênê and that of the non-Aryan East. We must, in accordance with previous interpretation, regard the two calves as representing the new moon and the full moon, which draw their strength from the decreasing and increasing crescent moon, the animal being represented as male in accordance with the sex of the Moon-god.

XXX.

Another remarkable gold ornament is described by Schliemann as 'two stags lying down, with long three-branched horns, leaning with the necks against each other, and turning the head in opposite directions [like the Assyrian Unicorn-goats in No. III.], but so that the horns of both touch each other, and seem intended to form a sort of crown.' [75] Here again the peculiar design shows a unity of origin, although very likely the maker of the Mykenean example had no thought of lunar symbolism. The 'stags' are small spotted fallow-deer, and each has but one horn, in which are three tines; in fact, the treatment of the horn is precisely similar to that of the same animal in Assyrian representations. [76] The eye, too, is very prominent. [77]

XXXI.

Another example given by Schliemann [78] shows two spotted, couchant, bull-like, prominent-eyed Unicorns, the horn in each case being treated exactly as in the last example, their necks touching, but the head of each reverted in the usual special manner.

XXXII.

The next example from Schliemann [79] shows a queer-looking animal with the head of an ass, and bear's paws, and one long horn with several tines. It is described as 'a Stag, of an alloy of silver and lead.'

XXXIII.

Lion and Unicorn fighting (?). [80]

The above instances by no means exhaust the appearances of the Unicorn in archaic art, and at the same time show that the idea of such a creature was familiar in Babylonia, Assyria, Egypt, Asia Minor and Greece. Many points in the representations will become more suggestive in the course of the enquiry; meanwhile it may be noticed as a general result that;—

I.   The Monster-unicorn is not lunar.
II. The Bovine-unicorn is more or less lunar.
III. The Unicorn-antelope, except perhaps in Egypt, and the Unicorn-goat, are distinctly and essentially lunar.
IV. The Unicorn is very frequently represented as attacking or attacked by the Lion.

Inman remarks that the Bull (whose frequent unicornic character he does not observe), and the Lion 'amongst the Assyrians, *occupied much the same place as the lion and the unicorn do in modern heraldry.*' [81]

Footnotes

1 Smith, *C.A.G.* 109.

2 For a comparison between the Babylonian and Norse ideas on this subject, vide R. B. Jr., *R.M.A.*, sec. xiv. The Seven Wicked Spirits of the Babylonian myth may be paralleled exactly with Seven Evil Personages of the Norse mythology, thus;—

BABYLONIAN.	NORSE.
Scorpion-of-rain.	Midhgardhsormer (the World-encircling Serpent, primarily cast from heaven as rain).
Thunderbolt.	Angurbodha ('Messenger of fear').
Leopard.	Fenrir (the nocturnal Wolf).
Serpent.	Nidhoggr ('Gnawing-serpent').
Watch-dog.	Garmr ('Swallower,' the hell-hound).
Tempest.	Beli ('Roarer')-Loki (Fire).
Evil-wind.	Egdir ('Eagle.' Aquila-aquilo).

I am unable here to pursue this very interesting subject (vide Lenormant, *Les Origines*, 520; Smith, *C.A.G.*, 99 *et seq.*).

3 Smith, *C.A.G.* 101.

4 *Ibid.* 114.

5 Vide R. B. Jr., *G.D.M.*, cap. IX. sec. iii., *Taurokerôs*.

6 Vide Lajard, *Culte de Mithra*, pl. xlvii.

7 Apud Inman, *Ancient Faiths*, i. 150.

8 I do not always use this term in its strictest sense, *i.e.*, looking towards the sinister.

9 *C.A.G.* 112.

10 This animal may be one of the hunter-god's 'four divine dogs,' Ukkumu ('Despoiler'), Akkulu ('Devourer'), Iksuda ('Capturer'), and Iltebu ('Carrier-away'). For the Sun-god to be dog-attended is no novelty. Vide the Vedic Yams (R. B. Jr., *R.M.A.*, Appendix C. 5). It is to be observed that this conventional position, standing on an animal, reappears further west, *e.g.*, at Pterion, in Asia Minor (vide Waring, *Ceramic Art in Remote Ages*, pl. xxxix, fig. 16), where a figure said to be the goddess Anaitis, holding a crescent-topped staff and accompanied by a salient unicornic animal, stands on the back of a leopard-like animal, and is followed by an attendant who stands on the back of a dog. Here, again, crescent and unicorn are seen in close connexion.

11 As to the triple aspect of the moon, vide secs. VI., IX.

12 For the connexion between the Unicorn and the Tree, vide sec. XII., subsec. 3.

13 No. III.

14 *C.A.G.* 35.

15 Lajard, *Culte de Vénus*, pl. xxii. fig. 3. A. carnelian cylinder.

16 Vide Prof, Rawlinson, A.M. ii.

17 A cylinder (ap. King, *A.G.R.* vol. ii. pl. ii. fig. 6).

18 Vide sec. XII. subsec. 3.

19 Vide No. III.

20 Vide a similar figure in Prof. Rawlinson's *A.M.* ii. 16.

21 The Akkadian Enzuna, the waxing-moon. Cf. *Deut.* xxxiii. 14; 'The precious things put

forth by the moon.'

22 Cf. the solar voyager Kibirra-Izdubar, the golden Phoenician Chrysôr, who 'was the first man who fared in ships;' Melqarth, the solar Tyrian hero, who sails to the farthest regions of the West (vide *G.D.M.* cap. XI. sec. i.); the Aryan Fish-sun (Apollôn Delphinios), Frog-sun, etc. So 'when the sun had set Oannês used to retire again into the sea, and pass the night in the deep' (Alexander Polyhistor, ap. Cary, *Ancient Fragments*, 56). The Zodiacal Capricorn, which appears portrayed much as at present on a uranographic Babylonian stone of the twelfth century B.C. now in the British Museum (vide Professor Rawlinson, *A.M.* ii. 574), originally represented the Fish-sun climbing goat-like up the eastern steep.

23 Lajard, *Culte de Vénus*, pl. iii. fig. 8.

24 Vide No. XXII. 2.

25 Layard, ap. Inman, *Ancient Faiths*, vol. i. fig. 66.

26 Vide sec. XII. subsec. 2.

27 *A.M.* iii. 339-40.

28 This contest between Day and Night, is shown farther west on coins of Akanthos, where the lion-sun seizes the bull of night which is apparently unicornic. In later idea the design embraces the contest between the principles of destruction and renewal (vide *G.D.M.* i. 387).

29 *A.M.* 354.

30 Vide No. XIX. 4.

31 Ap. King, *A.G.R.* vol. ii. pl. i. fig. 1.

32 *Ibid.* fig. 7.

33 Perhaps this tree may, as Mr. King suggests, have been also originally connected with the cult of the Vedic Soma, the Iranian Haoma, the Omomi of Plutarch, and the Horn of Anquetil du Perron (vide R. B. Jr., *G.D.M.* cap. IX. sec. ii. *Theoinos*).

34 On the question whether a cow or a bull is represented, and why, vide No. XXIX.

35 King, *A.G.R.* vol. ii. pl. ii. fig. 4.

36 Vide Nos. II. III. IX.

37 Vide *G.D.M.* cap. IX. sec. iii. *Taurokerôs*.

38 'Late late yestreen I saw the new moone
Wi' the auld moone in hir arme.'
(*Ballad of Sir Patrick Spens*, 7.)

39 *Numismata Hellenica*, ii. 144.

40 Vide *G.D.M.* i. 388.

41 Vide Humphrey, *Coin Collectors' Manual*, pl. i. figs. 2, 4, 5. He well observes, 'the type of the bull and lion would appear to have been derived from Persia or Assyria' (vol. i. 13).

42 Vide Rawlinson, *A.M.* iii. fig. 87, p. 305.

43 This is a specially interesting feature; the Scorpion, as I have shown elsewhere (*The Archaic Solar-Cult of Egypt*), was originally a type of darkness. The darkness in archaic idea first stings the Sun to death, and then when kosmic order is realised, guards it. This is the basis of the Akkadian myth of the giant 'Scorpion-men' found by Izdubar. 'At the rising of the sun and the setting of the sun, they guard the sun' (*Izdubar Tablets*, No. ix., ap. Smith, *C.A.G.* 250).

44 Rawlinson, *A.M.* iii. 334.

45 *Symbolik*, vol. v. fig. 8.

46 Vide p. 16, note 3.

47 Vide a Cylinder (*A.M.* ii. 16).

48 *Ibid.* i. 351.

49 *Ibid.* i. 521.

50 Rawlinson, *Herod.* ii. 225.

51 Rich, *Second Memoir on Babylon*, fig. 11.

52 Rawlinson, *A.M.* i. 265.

53 *Ibid.* 408.

54 *Recherches*, vol. i. pl. xv.

55 Vol. v. In voc. *Taurus*.

56 Vide R. B. Jr., *G.D.M.* i. 390. The Mardians were a Persian tribe (Herod. i. 125), whose name, according to Sir H. C. Rawlinson, signifies 'heroes,' and who occupied the mountain range south of Persepolis (vide Prof. Rawlinson, *Herod.* i. 345).

57 Vide *G.D.M.* ii. 122 *et seq.* In voc. *Serapis*.

58 Vide sec. IX.

59 *A.G.R.* vol. ii. pl. liii, fig. 1.

60 *Ib.* pl. xvi. fig. 1.

61 Aelianus, *Peri Zôôn*, vii. 48.

62 Clem. Alex. *Protrept.* ii. 38.

63 As to Athamas, vide *G.D.M.* i. 247 *et seq.* Sir G. W. Cox, whose candour is equal to his ability, now agrees with me that Athamas is identical with Tammuz (*Introd.* 67, note 2). M. Darmesteter connects the name with an Aryan root *ath*, whence Athênê, etc. (*O et A.* 55, note 2). The incidents of the myth will serve to solve philological doubts.

64 Taylor, in Calmet's *Dict.*, vol. V. xxii.

65 Lenormant, *Les Origines*, 570; vide sec. XII. subsec. 3.

66 Ap. Clermont-Ganneau, *L'Imagerie Phénicienne et la Mythologie Iconologique chez les Grecs*, 1880, pl. iv.

67 Vide Rawlinson, *Herod.* ii. 225.

68 Bunsen, *Egypt's Place*, i. 526.

69 *Ibid.* 568.

70 Pierret, *Essai sur la Mythologie Égyptienne*, 70.

71 *Ancient Egyptians*, edit. 1878, vol. ii. p. 93.

72 *M. & T.* fig. 175, p. 112.

73 Vide *Ibid.* fig. 315, p. 202.

74 Vide No. III.

75 *M & T.* fig. 264, p. 170.

76 Vide No. XIX.

77 Vide No. XIII.

78 *M. &. T.* fig. 264, p. 175.

79 *Ibid.* fig. 376, p. 257.

80 *Ibid.* fig. 470, p. 309; vide sec. XII., subsec. 2.

81 *Ancient Faiths*, i. 376.

IV
Deus Lunus

THE MOON-POWER, owing to the influence of the Greek Arte-mis-Selênê, the Latin Diana-Luna, is generally feminine in our thoughts; but this aspect, though also occasionally occurring else-where, *e.g.*, in Peru, is really exceptional. Thus among the Germanic nations the moon is masculine and the sun feminine. It is the daughter of Sôl, the Norse Sun-goddess, who in the regenerated world 'shall ride on her mother's track when the gods are dead'; [1] and it is the god Mâni, [2] who at Ragnarok, 'the-Twilight-of-the-gods,' shall be devoured by the Wolf of darkness, Managarmr, 'Moon-swallower,' a reduplication of the terrible wolf Fenrir. [3]

In Egypt again, 'Chons is the personification of the moon, and in this character he is called Chonsaah or Chons the moon. His name seems to mean "the chaser," or "pursuer,"' [4] the Unicorn who, as we shall see, [5] chases the Lion-sun. Another Kamic-lunar personage is Teti (Thoth), the weighing and measuring god, lord of knowledge and writing. [6] 'The crescent is found followed by the figure of Thoth in several hieroglyphic legends, with the phonetic name Aah.' [7]

'The Arabs to this day, consider the moon masculine, and not feminine.' [8]

'In Sanskrit the most current names for the moon, such as Kandra, Soma, Indu, Vidhu, are masculine. The names of the moon are frequently used in the sense of month, and these and other names for month retain the same gender.' [9]

In Asia Minor was widely established the cult of the Moon-god Mên, [10] the Lunus of the Romans, who, to a great extent suppressed his ritual.

The Babylonian and Assyrian Moon-god is Sin, [11] whose name probably appears in Sinai. The expression, 'From the origin of the god Sin,' was used by the Assyrians to mark remote antiquity; because as chaos preceded order, so night preceded day, and the enthrone-ment of the moon as the Night-king marks the commencement of the annals of kosmic order.

The Akkadian Moon-god, who corresponds with the Semitic Sin, is Aku, 'the Seated-father,' as chief supporter of kosmic order, styled 'the-Maker-of-brightness,' En-zuna, 'the-Lord-of-growth,' and Idu, the-Measuring-lord,' [12] the Aïdês of Hesychios. [13] Idu is the equiv-alent of the Assyrian Arkhu, 'month,' Heb. Yerakh; and is expressed in archaic Babylonian by the ideograph ⟨◄◄⟩ = the circle, (solar or) lunar + ⟨⟨⟨ (10 + 10 + 10), i.e., the thirty days of the month. ⟨⟨⟨ also stands for the Moon-god as the god-thirty. Amongst the Finns Kuu is 'the male god of the moon,' [14] and exactly corre-sponds with A-ku. It is singular to find also Kua as a moon-name in Central Africa. [15]

'Among the Mbocobis of South America, the moon is a man and the sun his wife.' [16]

Amongst the Mexicans, Metztli, the Moon, was a hero. [17]

According to an Australian legend, 'Mityan, the Moon, was a native cat [male], who fell in love with some one else's wife, and was driven away to wander ever since.' [18]

'The Khasias of the Himalaya say that the moon [male] falls monthly in love with his mother-in-law, who throws ashes in his face, whence his spots.' [19]

Ra Vula, the Figian Moon, is male. [20]

The Ahts of Vancouver's Island regard 'the Moon as husband and the Sun as wife.' [21]

In Japan 'the Moon-god was worshipped under the form of a fox.' [22]

The Unicorn is represented as male, being 'maiden' with respect to chastity. [23]

Footnotes

1   Vide R. B. Jr., *R.M.A.* sec. xvii.

2   Proto-Aryan root *ma*, to measure, whence Sk. *mâs*, Zend *mâo*, Lith. *menu*, Gk. *mênê*, in Ulfilas *mêna*, Anglo-Sax. *môna*, Swedish *mane*, Eng. *moon*. These words, except perhaps *mâo*, are all masculine. From the same root come the Sk. *mâsa*, Goth. *menoth*, Anglo-Sax. *monâdh*, Gk. *mên*, Lat. *mensis*, Eng. *month*. The Moon is the Month-measurer.

3   Vide *R.M.A.*, secs. xii. xv. 'The sun and moon were addressed as *Frau* and *Herr*, Domina and Dominus' (Thorpe, *Northern Mythology*, i. 281).

4   Dr. Birch in Wilkinson's *Anct. Egyptians*, iii. 174-5.

5   Sec. XII. subsec. 2.

6   Vide *G.D.M.* ii. 121 *et seq.* In voc. *Teti*.

7   Wilkinson, *Anct. Egyptians*, iii. 105.

8   *Ibid.* 39.

9   Prof. Max Müller, *L.S.L.* i. 7.

10 Vide Strabo, XII. iii. 31; viii. 14.

11 'Sin is used for the Moon in Mendaean and Syriac at the present day; and it was the term used for Monday by the Sabæans as late as the ninth century' (Prof. Rawlinson, *A.M.* i. 124, note 5).

12 *Id*, a measure, + *U*, lord.

13 Ἀϊδῶ Ἀϊδὴς· ἡ σελήνην παρὰ Χαλδαίοις (Hesychios, in voc.).

14 Lenormant, *Chaldean Magic*, 249.

15 Vide Tylor, *P.C.* ii. 272.

16 *Ibid.* i. 260.

17 *Ibid.* 262.

18 *Ibid.* 320.

19 *Ibid.*

20 *Ibid.* 321.

21 *Ibid.* ii. 272.

22 Vide Tylor, *P.C.* ii. 273.

23 Cf. Shakspere:—
    'Thou maiden youth, be vanquished by a maid.'
    (1 *Hen.* VI., A. iv. S. 7.)

V
The Lunar phases

THE SUCCESSION of apparent alterations in the form of the moon presents a phenomenon so remarkable as necessarily to have attracted the attention and careful observation of man from the earliest period. With the Greeks the phases were named;—

I. The New Moon. *Noumênia*, which because in the same line or path with the Sun, is called Synodos.

II. The Young Moon. *Nea Selênê*. Time in the month, *Protê Phasis*, 'the First Appearance;' a slender crescent seen a short time after sunset.

III. The Increasing Crescent. *Hexagônos*, 'Six-angled,' as having run $1/6$th of its course.

IV. The Half Moon. *Hemitomos*, 'Cut-in-twain.' [1] Also called *Tetragônos*, as having four equal angles in its circuit, ¼th of which it has now passed.

V. The Increasing Moon. *Amphikurtos*, 'Curved-on-each-side.' Also called *Trigônos*, 'Triangular,' for were an equilateral triangle drawn from its starting-point, the present position would be the apex, ⅓rd of its course being now passed.

VI. The Full Moon. *Panselênos*. Also called *Dichomênia*, the 'Month-divider.'

VII.   The Decreasing Moon. *Amphikurtos, Trigonos.*

VIII.   The Second Half-Moon. *Hemitomos*, etc.

IX.   The Decreasing Crescent. *Menoeidês*, 'Crescent-shaped,' Lat. *Lunatus.*

X.   The Old Moon. *Enê Selênê.* Time in the month,—*Eschatê Phasis*, 'the Last Appearance.' A slender crescent.

The corresponding Latin names are;—

I.   The New Moon. *Novilunium*, which being invisible is called *Luna Silens*, and the time styled *Congressus cum Sole.*

II.   The Young Moon. *Nova Luna.* Period,—*Prima Phasis.*

III.   The Increasing Crescent. *Primus sextilis aspectus.*

IV.   The Half Moon. *Luna dividua, semiplena, bisecta. Prima quadratura.*

V.   The Increasing Moon. *Luna gibba*, 'the Humpbacked Moon.' *Luna in triquetro.*

VI.   The Full Moon. *Plenilunium.* Also *Oppositio*, the Moon being now opposite the Sun; *Luna totilunis, Medius mensis.*

VII.   The Decreasing Moon. *Luna gibba.*

VIII.   The Second Half Moon. *Luna dividua*, etc. *Secunda quadratura.*

TX.   The Decreasing Crescent. *Corniculata, falcata, curvata in cornua.*

X.   The Old Moon. *Ultima phasis.*

The epithets *menoeides, corniculata*, and the like, apply to any crescent phase of the moon. During the first half of its course the moon is *Selênê auxanominê, Luna crescens*, the Waxing moon; during the last half, *Selênê phthinousa, Luna decrescens, senescens*, the Waning moon. As the Crescent-moon is nearest the Sun, [2] so it is the crescent-moon that is represented with the young sun in its arms; [3] and the crescent-moon is also the mother of the old moon and of the full moon. This is shown in the east window of Herringfleet Church, Suffolk, [4] where the crescent surrounds the full invisible moon, in the circle of which is the face of an angel. The Unicorn-goat during the first half of its career bounds forward from the sun, at which and the earth it looks back, and hence is regardant; during the second half of its career it bounds back towards the sun, looking round to the point whence it has begun to return. [5]

The lunar phases received the greatest attention from Babylonian and Akkadian observers; but we are not yet in a position to formulate results, as in the case of the Classical languages. Every position and alteration was more or less portentous, the system of portents being founded on the triple basis of (1) actual natural incident, (2) anthropomorphic analogy, or (3) synchronous occurrence. 'The left horn' and 'the right horn' of the moon are both mentioned, but it is also described as having, like the Unicorn, a single horn. Thus we read—*Ina ri-ib Karnu* [6] *la ikh-khi-rav*. 'Owing to rain, *the Horn* was not visible.' [7] Another passage states, 'Venus is in the ascendant; and (is) on *the Horn of*—' [8] Prof. Sayce supplies 'the Sun.' Rather, I think, 'the Moon.' Again,—'A dark cloud covered *the Horn*.' [9] Again, 'the moon *in its horn* like the stars is white.' [10] The Crescent-moon is called *Karunu*, 'Horned.'

Footnotes

1   Some tribes consider this to be the act of the angry Sun, an illustration of the hostility of Lion and Unicorn.

2   Cf. *W.A.I.*, III. lviii. 5: 'The Moon the Sun overtook, and with it had lingered. (It is) horned' (ap. Prof. Sayce in *T.S.B.A.* iii. 212).

3   Vide Lenormant in *Chaldean Magic*, Device on back; Inman, *Ancient Faiths*, ii. 261, 325; Moor, *Hindu Pantheon*, pl. ii. Sectarial Marks; *inf. sec* VIII.

4   Vide *Proceedings of the Society of Antiquaries*, vi. 459; vide also sec. III. No. XIV.

5   Vide sec. III. No. III.

6   The ideograph shows the horned cap of the early Babylonians. *Karnu*, Heb. *keren*, which reappears in the Gk. KRoNos, for KaRNos ('There is no such being as Κρόνος in Sanskrit.'—professor M. Müller, *Selected Essays*, 1881, vol. i. 460), Apollòn-Karneios, etc., singularly resembles the Lat. *cornu*, Eng. *horn*, as the Gk. *keras* does the Heb. *keren*; but Semitic and Aryan words must not be allied without the most stringent proofs.

7   *W.A.I.* III. li. 9, ap. Prof. Sayce.

8   *T.S.B.A.* iii. 199.

9   *Ibid*. 226.

10   *Ibid*. 297.

VI
Hekatê

WITH THE LUNAR phases is closely connected the mysterious goddess, Hekatê, 'the-Far-shooting,' whose Aryan name, like the epithets Hekatos, Hekatebolos, Telephos, Telephassa, etc., describes
'the far-reaching action of the solar or lunar rays.' [1] Unmentioned in
the Homerik Poems, she appears before us in the pages of Hesiod [2]
as an august figure, daughter of Perses [3] and Asteria, the star-lighted
splendour of space, honoured above all by Zeus and the other gods
although a Titanic being of a race earlier than the completed Pantheon of Olympos. Sole-begotten, a survival of the fittest, endowed
with a triple dominion in earth, sea, and heaven, she sits in the seat
of judgment beside kings, crowns whom she will with victory in war
and in the games, grants wealth and honour, is patron of riders and
mariners, and is generally Kourotrophos, 'a Nursing-mother.' This
remarkable personage, whose character seems more complicated
than that of an ordinary Aryan divinity, and who receives the utmost
respect from the race of Zeus to which she does not belong, presents
a striking analogy with the august Moon-god of the Euphrates Valley,
sole-begotten 'amongst the stars that have a different birth,' wise
and ancient ruler of the sea, connected with growth, with the horse,
and, as we shall see, with the Unicorn, and in some way or other of a
triple character; Hesiod gives her dominion in earth, sea, and heav-

en, whilst others give her sway in heaven, earth, and underworld. True she has received an Aryan name, and in accordance with the lunar feelings of the Greeks, is represented as a goddess; but these circumstances are by no means conclusive on the question of her origin. I am unable, however, to pursue the enquiry here, suffice it to draw attention to the parallel. The cult of the goddess appears to have entered Greece from the direction of Thrakê. [4]

The very important element of triplicity is a remarkable link between the Euphratean Moon-god, Hekatê [5] and the Unicorn. The Moon-god Sin, as we have seen, [6] is represented by the three tens from the natural circumstance that his course was completed in about thirty days. This is one aspect of his triplicity, and tends to bring his trigonic phase into greater prominence; but he was also regarded by the Babylonians as having a threefold movement, 'one in longitude, one in latitude, and one in an orbit,' [7] and here is a second aspect of triplicity. But ere men calculated the course of the moon, or considered its real or supposed different movements, they observed the orb itself, and noticed its three phases or forms—Crescent-moon, Half-moon, and Full-moon. 'Cum tribus pingebatur, faciebus, inquit Cleomedes, quia veteres tres in luna figuras observabant, bicornis scilicet lunae, mediae et plenae.' [8] In the *Argonautika*, [9] a poem of late date, but to which in common with numerous other apocryphal productions the name of Orpheus [10] has been attached, Hekatê Triformis appears as Horse, Dog, and Snake. Sir G. W. Cox connects the Horse with the Full-moon, the Snake with the Waxing-moon, and the Dog with the Waning-moon; but, whilst this connexion is anything but obvious, another view of these phases will I think be admitted to be the correct one. And here let me call special attention to one of the most venerable relics in England, a drawing of a portion of which forms the Frontispiece of this Monograph, namely, the ivory horn of Ulf now in the vestry of York Minster. 'An inscription in Latin upon the horn states that Ulphus, prince of the Western parts of Deira, originally gave it to the church of St. Peter, together with all his lands and revenues. Camden, in his Britannia, mentions this horn, and quotes an ancient authority for an account of the donation of which it served as a token. The church holds by this horn several estates of great value, not far eastward from the city of York, and which are still called Terrae Ulphi.' [11] And now upon this famous Horn we find both Hekatê Triformis and the Unicorn; the Horned-horse is palpably the Crescent-moon; the Snake or Serpent is the emblem of the rays of light from the Full-moon, the Gorgô Medousa; [12] and the Dog, whose head and neck only appear, represents the Half-moon. The Dog may be also connected with the New or Invisible-moon. Pausanias says that 'the Kolophonians sacrifice a *black* whelp to Enodios,' [13] *i.e.*, Hekatê, as goddess of cross-roads. The Unicorn of Ulf has the prominent eye before noticed in unicornic representations, [14] and which refers to the increasing moon soon to be full. The horn, it will be observed, is fast in the Sacred Tree, [15] and this feature of the myth I shall have occasion subsequently [16] to notice particularly. Suffice it to remind the reader here that dark groves were sometimes sacred to Hekatê, as *e.g.*, near Lake Avernus in Lower Italy. [17] Black female lambs were also offered to the goddess. [18]

It is evident that this triple-moon-phase, Unicorn-horse, Serpent and Dog, familiar alike to the artist of the Horn and to the writer of the *Argonautika* (not to mention others), is of a high antiquity. Hekatê has a triple power in 'Hesiod,' the Euphratean Moon-god is equally connected with triplicity; [19] but the chief point in the present investigation is that the Unicorn, whom we have seen in Babylonian art in the closest connexion with the lunar power, is shown by this venerable Horn to be beyond all contradiction the undoubted emblem of the crescent-moon.

Elsewhere I have observed, 'Hellenik divinities whose shapes are grotesque, monstrous or unhuman, are invariably not indigenous. Apparent exceptions to this canon, such, for instance, as the Horse-headed Dêmêtêr of Phigaleia, or the Arkadian Pan, on careful examination, serve only to confirm it.' [20] After noticing 'the Four-faced Karthaginian Baal,' 'the solar Time-king in his four changing seasons,' I remarked;—

'In the Kerameikos, at a place where three ways met, stood a four-headed Dionysiak statue, the work of the sculptor Telesarchides. It has been frequently said that Hekatê and Hermes derive their occasional triplicity, and other unanthropomorphic adjuncts, from presiding over places where three roads met and the like. But although in later times these ideas were to some extent connected, and though the statue of a tri-kephalik or tetra-kephalik divinity might indeed with much propriety be erected where three or four roads met; yet the previous supposed character of the personage would occasion the act, the idea of many heads would not spring

from that of cross-roads. That the heads in origin were quite inde-
pendent of the roads, is well shown in the instances before us, in
which a *four*-headed god presided where *three* ways met.' [21] Other
epithets of Hekatê, such as Trioditis, [22] Triceps, Tergeminus, Trivia,
etc., require no further remark; and with the degradation of the goddess, the process by which she at length becomes a demon-witch,
culminating in the Shaksperian Hekatê, I am not here concerned,
nor in the present investigation can I refer further to the Moon-dog.

Footnotes

1   Rev. Sir G. W. Cox, *Introd.* 66.
2   *Theogonia*, 409-52.
3   Vide secs. VII. XII. subsec. 3.
4   Cf. Paus. II. xxx. 1.
5   'Tergeminam Hecaten, tria virginis ora Dianae' (Vergil, iv. 511). According to Pausanias, 'Alkamenes [cir. B.C. 420] first made for the Athenians the statue of Hekatê with three bodies joined in one' (Paus. II. xxx. 1). There was also a 'three-handed Hekatê' (Sir G. W. Cox, *M.A.N.* i. 370). The statue of Alkamenes was not unanthropomorphic, but three female figures addorsed (vide *G.D.M.* i. 420), like the example given by Montfaucon (vol. i. pt. i. pl. xc. fig. 5), and frequently since reproduced.
6   Sec. IV.
7   Prof. Sayce, in *T.S.B.A.* iii. 147.
8   Montfaucon, vol. i. pt. i. p. 152.
9   V. 975 *et seq.*; vide Sir G. W. Cox, *M.A.N.* ii. 142.
10 Probably 'the Vedic Ribhu or Arbhu, a name which seems at a very early period to have been applied to the sun' (Sir G. W. Cox, *Introd.* 191; cf. R. B. Jr., *G.D.M.* i. 10).
11 Winkle, *Cathedral Churches*, i. 62.
12 Sec. VII.
13 Paus. III. xiv. 9. It is to be noticed that he uses a masculine form of the name of the goddess. Euripides calls her Enodia.
14 Sec. III. Nos. V. XIII. XXX.
15 Cf. the instances of Unicorn and Tree, sec. III.
16 Sec. XII. subsec. 3.
17 Vide A. S. Murray, *Manual of Mythology*, 78.
18 Plutarch, *Quaest. Rom.* xlix.
19 If the three-headed Lion-god of Meroe (vide Rawlinson, *Herod.* ii. 35), who has four arms (vide my remarks on the four-armed Lakedaimonian Apollôn, *G.D.M.* i. 359 *et seq.*) be solar, we should have an instance of solar triplicity also. The Triform Hekatê appears at times on Roman lamps (vide Birch, *Ancient Pottery*, 507, 511. As to these representations of the goddess, vide also Petersen, *Archaeologisch-epigraphische Mittheilungen aus Oesterreich*, vol. iv. pt. ii.).
20 *G.D.M.* i. 359. In this work I have examined many instances of unanthropomorphic divinities which appear in Hellenik regions.
21 *G.D.M.* i. 362.
22 *Orphik Hymn*, i. l.

VII
Medousa the Gorgô

FROM THE TRIPLE-MOON and the Unicorn-horse-moon I pass on
to the Serpentine-full-moon, the victim of the solar Perseus, another
version of the oft-recurring story. Careful study of the Homerik
Poems reveals the intrinsically archaic nature and high antiquity of
the majority of their ideas, and in the consideration of any mythic
personage a passage in Homer, if available, almost always supplies
an excellent starting-point. It is generally, but not quite accurately
stated that 'Homer knows only one Gorgo.' The passages are as
follows;—

'On it [the *aigis* of Athenaiê] was a Gorgeian head of a dreadful
portent.' [1]

'Hektôr, having the eyes of a Gorgô.' [2]

'An awful-looking Gorgô' [3] was the device upon the shield of
Agamemnôn.

Odysseus fears 'lest Persephoneia from Hades should send
a Gorgeian head of a dreadful portent.' [4] From these passages we
gather:—

1. That whilst there was certainly one Gorgô, there may also
   have been others.
2. That its eye constituted the chief terror of the appearance. [5]

3. That this appearance, originally portentous, [6] became, or was considered to be, monstrous. [7]

4. That, though having a bright eye, it is connected with Darkness and the Underworld. And

5. Was used heraldically as arms upon a shield.

Fick would connect the obscure word Gorgô with the European root *garg*, 'to cry,' and compares the Sk. *garj*, 'to emit a deep sound;' [8] but the idea of sound is so truly out of place in the myth (a circumstance which we are bound to consider), that I am compelled to reject this derivation. I had deemed the term as possibly an intensive variant of *orgê*, 'natural impulse,' primarily 'swelling' (first physics, then meta-physics), as applied to the swollen, full-faced Moon; for from Homer alone it is not very difficult to gather that Gorgô = Luna. But the detail of a myth is the true test by which to try various etymologies of the name of its protagonist, especially when in the abstract several distinct derivations appear to have an almost equal claim to acceptance. Now the Gorgon-power (as will more fully appear) = Nocturnal-darkness + Moon, not darkness merely or the moon merely. Darkness, it will be remembered, is frequently (like Chaos) depicted in monstrous form; but especially is it a Devourer or Swallower. [9] The Proto-Aryan root *gar*, 'to swallow, gulp,' appears in the intensive form *gargar*, [10] the Gk. variant of which would be Gorgô, the earliest form of the word in that language. Gorgô is 'the Swallower,' the devouring darkness which has a bright head—the Moon, a head capable of being cut off. Hence the combined beauty and horror (hideousness) of the Gorgô, a hideousness which does not arise in the first instance from the lunar-serpent-rays, and hence *the open mouth*, so marked a feature in the Gorgoneion and one not in the least lunar. Mr. Dennis observes;—

The most remarkable type on the coins of Populonia is the Gorgoneion; not here "the head of the fair-cheeked Medusa" [11]—

"A woman's countenance with serpent locks,"

as it is represented by the sculptors of later Greece and of Etruria; but a monstrous fiend-like visage, with snaky hair, gnashing tusks, and tongue lolling out of

"The open mouth that seemed to containe
A good full peck within the utmost brim,
Appearing *like the mouth* of Orcus griesly grim." [12]

From this open mouth issue two huge curved teeth, the lunar horns. The protruded tongue and gnashing teeth were familiar to the author (probably Hesiod [13]) of the *Aspis Herakleous*. [14] And this leads us to the Hesiodik phase of the myth, according to which [15] there are three Gorgones (= Hekatê Triformis), Medousa 'the Ruler' (= the King or Queen-moon), Stheinô or Sthenô 'the Strong' (= the general Nocturnal-potency), and Euryalê 'the Wide-wandering' (= the Moon 'wandering companionless' [16]), a phase which corresponds with the solar Bellerophôn in the same Aleian Field. [17] Do not hastily charge the intricate myth with inconsistency. The Night is dark and not-dark, lunar and not-lunar; and so is the Gorgô; so are the Gorgones. And that the Gorgô is one as well as three, is shown clearly by a writer as late as Euripides. [18] The home of the Gorgones lies as of course in or beyond the western darkness; [19] with the Euemerism which first connected them with Libyê [20] as a western region, and has subsequently identified them with apes of some kind, gorilla or ourang-oötan, I am not here concerned. An early Vase shows the solar Herakles, who for the purpose is the equivalent of the solar Perseus, 'killing the threefold Gorgon.' [21]

As Hekatê is Perseis or Perseia [22] and daughter of Perses, so Hekatos is Perseus, 'the solar hero, son of Zeus (heaven), in the form of a gleaming golden shower, and his son Perses is the mythic sire of the Persians, the lords of the "sun-stricken plains" [23] of the East.' [24] Perseus naturally engages to attack the Gorgô as the Lion the Unicorn; and assisted by Athenê (the Dawn-light) and Hermes (the Wind-power upon the clouds [25]), sets forth upon the perilous expedition. The helmet of Hades ('the Unseen') renders him invisible, *i.e.* the condition of the Nocturnal-sun as concealed in the Underworld; and from the two Graiai [26] he seizes the solar eye [27] and lunar tooth, [28] which he will not restore until they tell him where to find the implements necessary to complete his task. This eye and tooth the sisters are wont to hand from one to the other, *i.e.* from morn to eve, from eve to morn. The hero having obtained the other requisites, 'Hermes added the knife (*harpê*) with which he had cut off the head of Argos;' [29] and this same potency which put out the starry eyes, now puts out the lunar eye, or, to change the imagery, cuts off the bright head of the dark Gorgô; but the light veiled for a moment, soon reappears on the *aigis* of the Dawn-queen. The Sun has done the deed—technically called the Gorgotomy—but he has to fly, pursued by Euryalê, the Reappearing-moon; and Stheinô, whom Sir G. W. Cox well describes as 'the eternal abyss of darkness.' [30] The petrifying stare of Medousa is the moon-glare on the darkness when the colour, sound, and motion of the world of day have gone.

This myth alone might well form the subject of a monograph, but I can "here only notice one other of its many incidents—the weapon of Perseus, the *harpê*, in shape a sickle or scimetar. Now the tradition that this was the special weapon used on the occasion, is a very ancient one, for Pherekydes, B.C. 540, who 'according to the concurrent testimony of antiquity was the teacher of Pythagoras,' and 'did not receive instruction from any master but obtained his knowledge from the secret books of the Phoenicians,' [31] expressly names it as used by Perseus in the Gorgotomy. [32] It is the same 'portentous sickle' (πελώριον ἅρπην) which Kronos took in his right hand when he assailed Ouranos, [33] for one of 'his peculiar adjuncts is the crescent-shaped sickle, which he somewhat singularly holds over his head in a scene where he is receiving from Rhea the stone supposed to be Zeus.' [34] Lastly, we find that 'the scimetar with which Merodach [or Bel] is armed [when about to fight with the Dragon] is shown by the cylinders and bas-reliefs to have been of the shape of a sickle, and is therefore [as had also occurred to me] the same as the *harpê* or *khereb* with which the hero Perseus was armed.' [35] Now Bel and Merodach fight against chaos and also against darkness, and the chief weapon of the god who maintains nocturnal kosmic order is, as of course, the sickle-shaped moon. Perseus, in accordance with the Principle of Reduplication above noticed, armed with the crescent-moon cuts off the Gorgô-head or full-moon; just as another mighty Babylonio-Akkadian divinity is described as being armed with the sun. [36] It is evident therefore that Perseus, who was supposed to have slain the sea-monster at Joppa, and who in a passage of Herodotos, difficult to explain, is said to have had a temple and ritual in Egypt, [37] was more or less connected with the non-Aryan East. Lenormant [38] gives an extract from a Babylonian Fragment of which he says, 'C'est le prototype de l'histoire de Persée et d'Andromède;' and he thinks that Perseus may be another variant form of the word represented by the Parsoudos of Ktesias, and is therefore in origin a Babylonian name. Very likely; but I do not doubt that it is also an Aryan name, that is to say, here probably, as in many other instances, an Aryan and a non-Aryan name, of somewhat similar sound, have become united like a double star. The sire of Andromedê, [39] Kepheus the Aithiop king and son of Belos, [40] is a personage altogether non-Aryan and Euphratean; and Hellanikos, B.C. 490-10, chief of the Greek logographers, mentions Kepheus and the Kephenians (Ethiopians or Kushites) in connexion with Babylon. [41]

Lastly, in the dread Gorgô, originally Darkness + Moon, then more distinctly lunar, we have the origin of the myth of the Face in the Moon. We know otherwise that this myth was archaic, for Epigenes of Sikyôn, 'the most ancient writer of tragedy,' [42] in a lost work called *The Poetry of Orpheus*, says that the Theologer called 'the moon Gorgonian on account of the face in it;' [43] and Serapiôn, an Alexandrine physician of the third century B.C., thought that 'the Face seen in the moon is the soul of the Sibylla.' [44] According to the doctrine set forth by Plutarch, [45] evil souls, on attempting to enter the tranquil lunar region, are driven away by the dread Face in the Orb. [46]

With respect to Gorgonian art, Sir G. Wilkinson is of opinion that 'the monster Medusa evidently derived its form from the common Typhonian figure of Egypt;' [47] and M. Clermont-Ganneau, in a most interesting work, has elaborated a theory which connects a beautiful female Gorgon with Hathor and Tanit, and a hideous male Gorgon with the Kamic Bes. [48]

Speaking of Etruscan temple-tombs, Mr. Dennis observes, 'The pediments terminate on each side in a volute, within which is a grim, grinning face, *with prominent teeth*, a Gorgon's head, a common sepulchral decoration.' [49] On the hollowed bottom of the famous Etruscan bronze lamp in the Museum of Cortona is 'a huge Gorgon's face, all horror. The visage of a fiend, *with eyes starting from their sockets, a mouth stretched to its utmost, with gnashing tusks*—and the whole rendered more terrible by a wreath of serpents bristling around it.' [50] Well may Mr. Dennis add, 'It is a libel on the fair face of Dian, to say that this hideous visage symbolises the moon.' This difficulty I have fully explained.

On the ceiling of a chamber in the cemetery of Perugia is 'an enormous Gorgon's head, hewn from the dark rock, with eyes upturned in horror, gleaming from the gloom, *teeth bristling whitely in the open mouth*, wings on the temples, and snakes knotted over the brow.' [51] The Etruscans evidently fully shared in the Akkadian horror of darkness.

On the back of the late Mr. Cooper's edition of Lenormant's *Chaldean Magic* is represented (I presume from some Chaldean original) a Gorgoneion, apparently a black face, radiate, with wide and open grinning mouth. This presents a remarkable combination of moon and darkness.

Greek vases were occasionally moulded in the shape of the leg of Gorgô. [52] A Vase in the British Museum [53] shows a Gorgô in connexion with Lions. She holds upon either side a lion by the fore paw; the lions standing on their hind legs, fling back their heads. The design may of course be mere sportive art, but it appears to be Assyrian in origin [54] and may signify the Gorgonian Night stationed harmoniously between two leonine Days.

Another Vase [55] shows Perseus, wearing the *petasos* and *talaria*, plunging the *harpê*, which he holds in his right hand, into the neck of the Gorgô, who has four wings, two snakes on each side of her head, and two round her waist. 'Her face has the usual Gorgon type, with curls symmetrically ranged [an Assyrian characteristic], and a wide, open mouth showing the teeth and tongue.' Another Vase [56] shows the rare design of Perseus flying over the Libyan mountains, pursued by Stheinô and Euryalê. 'The wild pursuit of the immortal Gorgons seems to be the chase of Darkness after the bright Sun who, with his golden sandals, just escapes their grasp as he soars into the peaceful morning sky.' [57]

In Canon Spano's very interesting work, *Mnemosine Sarda*

ossia Ricordi e memorie di varii Monumenti Antichi con altre rarita dell' isola de Sardegna (Cagliari, 1864), several good examples of the Gorgon-type are given, the most remarkable of which shows three Gorgon-faces radiate, with open mouths and protruded tongues, in a circle—the lunar orb. Here the three Gorgon sisters are connected with the one Moon.

Footnotes

1   *Ilias*, v. 741. The phase δεινοῖο πελώρου occurs again in the same connexion (*Od.* xi. 634). It is not necessary to render πέλωρ 'monster.' The essential meaning of the word is 'portent' (cf. *Il.* ii. 321: πέλωρα θεῶν, 'portents sent from the gods'). That which is portentous is often monstrous, the appearance of monsters being particularly connected with the anger of heaven.

2   *Il.* viii. 349.

3   *Ibid.* xi. 36.

4   *Od.* xi. 634-5.

5   Cf. the prominent unicorn-eye (sec. III. Nos. V. XIII. XXX).

6   'As when the sun new risen
    Looks through the horizontal misty air
    Shorn of his beams, or from behind the moon
    In dim eclipse disastrous twilight sheds.'
    Paradise Lost, i. 594-7.

7   As Hekatê.

8   *Wörterbuch*, i. 565. A *g* sound appears to have been considered suitable to express the increasing, rounded (cf. γογόλος), humpbacked *gib*-bous-moon. In Akkadian *gub* means 'to wax' as the moon (vide R. B. Jr., *Language and Theories of its Origin*, 1881, sec. xvi. Occult Imitation).

9   Vide my remarks on the unique Etruscan demon Tuchulcha (*R.M.A.* Appendix D) whose enormous open beak = 'the jaws of vacant darkness' (Tennyson, *In Memoriam*, xxxiv.).

10 Fick, *Wörterbuch*, i. 70; vide R. B. Jr., *R.M.A.* sec. xix, The Law of Reduplication.

11 Pindar, *Pyth.* xii. 28.

12 *C.C.E.* ii. 221. 'The Manducus, a symbolic effigy with gaping jaws, was borne aloft in Roman games and processions to represent the underworld' (Rev. Is. Taylor, *Etruscan Researches*, i. 121).

13 Vide Mahaffy, *Hist. of Clas. Gk. Lit.* 1880, i. 112-3.

14 Λίχμαζον δ᾽ ἄρα τώγε· μένει δ᾽ χάρασσον ὀδόντας (v. 235).

15 *Theog.* 278.

16 The true poet, whether a 'modern-ancient,' as Shakspere, Shelley, or Wordsworth; or an ancient-modern, like many a Kamic, Babylonian or Vedic bard of unknown name, takes essentially the same stand-point.

17 *Alê* is a homeless, endless roaming, the ceaseless journey of the heavenly bodies in the field of space.

18 *Iôn*, 989.

19 Γοργοὺς θ᾽, αἵ ναίουσι πέρην κλυτοῦ Ὠκεανοῖο,
    ἐσχατιῇ πρὸς νυκτὸς (*Theog.* 274-5). Vide my remarks on the Assyrian *eribu*, 'to descend' as the, sun, *ereb*, 'the west,' *arab*, *erebos*, originally the gloom after sunset, *Europé*, the western or sunset side of the world (*R.Z.* 17, note 2).

20 Herod. ii. 91; Diod. iii. 69; Paus. II. xxi. 6. According to an account given by Pausanias, Medousa, queen of the inhabitants near the Tritonian Lake, when opposing the

Peloponnesian army of Perseus, was slain in the night by stratagem. Perseus admiring her beauty, cut off her head to show it to the Greeks. Pausanias himself, however, prefers the account given by Proklos a Karthaginian, that Medousa was one of the wild men and women of Africa who, wandering northwards and assailing the inhabitants, was slain by Perseus, who is said to have been assisted by Athena because the goddess is worshipped near the Tritonian Lake. (For a notice of Athenê Tritogenaia, and the family of the Vedic Trita, vide R. B. Jr., *Poseidon*, sec. xx.) Medousa having thus become a wild woman, it is only another step to turn her into a gorilla, and this has been taken by the learned Dr. Levezon of Berlin.

21 Birch, *Ancient Pottery*, 193.
22 *Orphik Hymn*, i. 4.
23 Euripides, *Bakchai*, 14.
24 *G.D.M.* i. 279.
25 Vide Ruskin, *Q.A.* i. secs. xxv.–xxix.
26 'The well-clad Pephrêdô,' the evening-power, and 'Enyô clad-in-saffron-mantle,' the warlike (cf. Enyalios) dawn or morning-power, Krokopeplos like Eôs. The Graiai, the 'Gray,' Dawn and Gray Twilight, 'with fair faces, but hair gray from their birth'—how wonderfully the myth describes the fact—can originally have been but two.
27 This is an instance of the Principle of Reduplication in myths, for of course Perseus himself is the solar eye. Similarly Herakles with his arrows attacks Helios. These incidents are frequently the necessary results of anthropomorphism. As Mr. F. A. Paley remarks, 'It is the unconscious blending of two modes of representation' (*Origin of Solar Myths*, in the *Dublin Review*, July, 1879, p. 109).
28 Here the tooth is most undoubtedly the lunar crescent, a fact which is the absolute justification of my explanation of the teeth of the Gorgoneion, a view which might otherwise have appeared too fanciful or far-fetched.
29 Murray, *Manual of Mythology*, 248. For treatment of the famous myth of Hermes Argeiphontes, vide Ruskin, *Q.A.* i. 28; R. B. Jr., *G.D.M.* ii. 83; R. M. A, sec. iii.
30 *M.A.N.* ii. 350. Dr. Tylor (*P.C.* i. 318) appears to regard the Gorgons as in some way representing period, and remarks, 'The deathless past and future cannot save the ever-dying present.' The real basis of the myth, however, is purely physical.
31 Smith, *Dict. of Gk. and Rom. Biog. and Mythol.* In voc. Vide in illustration of this statement, Lenormant, *Les Origines*, Appendice III. Fragments de la Cosmogonie de Phérécyde.
32 Ἀποτέμνει τῇ ἅρπη κεφαλὴν (*Frag.* xxvi).
33 *Theog.* 179. Cf. the Homerik use of the same πέλωρ in this connexion, as above noticed (p. 47, note 1).
34 *G.D.M.* ii. 129. In this work I have illustrated the Semitic character of Kronos.
35 Prof. Sayce in Smith's *C.A.G.* 113.
36 'The sun of fifty faces, the lofty weapon of my divinity, I bear. The hero that striketh the mountains, the propitious sun of the morning, that is mine, I bear' (*Hymn*, ap. Sayce in *C.A.G.* 86).
37 Vide sec. XII. subsec. 3.

38 *Les Premières Civilisations*, ii. 24-5.
39 Perhaps originally Antar-ma-da, *i.e.*, 'Sky-cutting-from-Media,' or eastern dawn-light. Her mythic position authorises a non-Aryan explanation of her name. Names subsequently applied to elaborations, *e.g.*, constellations, were probably in numerous cases primarily applied to far simpler phenomena.
40 Herod. vii. 61, 150.
41 *Persika*, Frag. iii. The star-group of Kepheus, Kassiopeia, Andromedê and Perseus points to Chaldean influence.
42 Souidas, in voc. *Thespis*.
43 Ap. Clem. Alex. *Stromata*, v. 8.
44 *Ibid*. i. 15. Sibylla, *i.e.*, 'Council-of-Zeus,' is a general name given to various shadowy and prophetic females of Classical antiquity, to whom the composition of divers late and anonymous verses was attributed.
45 *Concerning the Face in the Moon's Orb*.
46 On this myth, vide Rev. S. Baring-Gould, *Curious Myths of the Middle Ages*, The Man in the Moon.
47 Rawlinson's *Herodotus*, ii. 125.
48 *L'Imagerie Phénicienne*, 136 *et seq.*
49 *C.C.E.* i. 199.
50 *Ibid*. ii. 404.
51 *C.C.E.* ii. 441-2.
52 Birch, *Ancient Pottery*, 169; vide sec. sec. III. Nos. IV. VI.
53 Vase Catalogue, No. 1852.
54 Vide
55 *Brit. Mus. Cat.*, No. 641.
56 Brit. Mus. Cat. No. 548.
57 Cox, *M.A.N.* i. 102.

VIII
Inô and Melikertes

IN THE MYTH of Inô and Melikertes we see no longer opposition between Day and Night, Sun and Moon, but kosmic harmony, the crescent-moon-goddess with the young sun in her arms. Inô, the daughter of Kadmos the 'Easterner,' [1] is married to Athamas, 'in Ionic Tammas,' [2] the Phoenician Tammuz, [3] the Akkadian Dumuzi, 'the Only son,' *i.e.*, the solitary Sun-god, Melqarth, who goes forth to hunt alone. [4] By him she becomes the mother of Melikertes, the Phoenician Melqarth, or 'City-king;' his reduplication—the sun of the next day; and when the raging Athamas—Herakles Mainomenos—in madness slays his eldest child by Inô, the latter with the infant Melikertes, leaps into the sea, and is subsequently known as Leukotheê, 'the White-goddess.' The obscure name Inô is probably a variant of Iuno, Juno, and from being a phase of Hêrê, 'the Gleaming-heaven,' she becomes the Queen-of-heaven, Lebhânâ, 'the Pale-shiner,' the White-moon-goddess, the horned Astartê, and as such she assists the storm-tossed Odysseus with her headband (*Kredemnon*), a moon-scarf of the lunar rays. [5] Such is 'Inô with-beautiful-ankle,' 'the moon walking in brightness,' whose kindly unicorn-horn drives away noxious things; the fostering mother who, like a Juno Matuta, nurtures the young Sun-god Dionysos, who is identical with Melqarth (Melek, Molekh), after the death of his own mother Semelê, [6] he being the chief of 'the precious things put forth by the moon.' Not far from the Phoenician settlement in Kythera [7] was 'a temple and oracle of Inô. They prophesy when asleep, since the goddess answers those who consult her by dreams. Water, pleasant to drink, flows from a sacred fount, and they call it the Fount of the Moon.' [8] According to an MS. Neo-Platonik Commentary of Olympiodoros on the *Phaidôn*, 'Inô is water, being marine.' Here is a preservation of a faint shadow of the truth, for the connexion between the moon and water is obvious; but the theory of Olympiodoros that the four daughters of Kadmos represent the four (so-called) elements, may be paralleled with the modern view of Rolle, [9] that they represent the four stages of intoxication. [10] The leap of Inô with the child into the sea was localised at the rock Molyris near Megara, [11] whence Melikertes was said to have been carried on a dolphin, like Apollôn Delphinios, the Fish-sun, to Korinth, here he had a curious labyrinthine shrine. [12]

Footnotes

1   Semitic Kedem, 'the East.'

2   K. O. Müller, *Orchomenos and dier Minyer*, 156.

3   'Athamas is the god Tammuz.' (Sir G. W. Cox, *Introd.* 67, Note 2.)

4   Vide *G.D.M.* ii. 293. M. Lenormant and Prof. Sayce have pointed out the correct reading of Jeremiah, xxii. 18: 'Ah me, my brother, and ah me, my sister! Ah me, Adonis, and ah me, his lady!'

5   *Od.* v. 333-56. I have fully treated of these various personages in the *G.D.M.* i. 246 *et seq.*; ii. 286 *et seq.*, and shall therefore only notice them briefly here.

6   *Apollod.* iii. 4.

7   At Athens was 'a shrine of Aphrodite Ouraniê. Ouraniê was revered first amongst the Assyrians; and after the Assyrians by the Kyprian Paphians, and by those of the Phoenicians who dwell at Askalôn in Palestine; and the Kythereans learnt from the Phoenicians to revere her' (Paus. I. xiv. 6).

8   *Ibid.* III. xxvi. 1.

9   *Culte de Bacchus*, iii. 318.

10   Sir G. W. Cox strangely remarks of Leukotheê that her 'name proclaims her as the open and glaring day' (*Introd.* 217). But the Glaring-day does not fly from the Raging-sun, or hold the Infant-sun in her arms; and is no more a nursing, nurturing mother than Athamas is such a sire.

11   Paus. I. xliv. 11.

12   *Ibid.* II, ii. 1

The Three-legged Ass of the Bundahis

THE NEXT PHASE of the Unicorn is, I think, a novel one, and will solve a previously-felt difficulty. In the Pahlavi [1] work, the *Bundahish* or *Bundahis*, [2] is a circumstantial account of a wonderful animal called 'the Three-legged Ass,' which, according to M. Darmesteter, [3] is a personification of cloud, storm, etc.; but whilst this hypothesis can never be demonstrated, I think on a review of the evidence the contrary will clearly appear. The writer states;—

'Regarding the three-legged ass they say, that it stands amid the wide-formed ocean, and its feet are three, eyes six, mouths nine, ears two and HORN ONE, body white, food spiritual, and it is right-eous.' [4]

This puzzle to commentators now at once becomes luminous. The triform, triquetric Moon stands amid the wide Oversea of heaven, the 'mare magnum sine fine,' and 'its feet are three.' To what other personage or phenomenon would this apply? To attempt to explain every detail in the late and elaborated, and possibly in part purely arbitrary, account would be very unsafe. Suffice it if the main outline comes out quite clearly. The Ass, a wise and sagacious animal, especially in Eastern idea, [5] has six eyes or two for each of the three phases; the Horse-Serpent-Dog-Moon has six eyes. There is some doubt about the word translated 'mouths;' it may mean 'testes,' and, if so, would connect the moon as usual with fertility and increase. The two ears may be the two ends of the horn, which is that of the lunar Unicorn. Its body is of course white—Leukotheê. From the archaic time of the Babylonian Moon-god Sin 'it is righteous,' nay, the leader of righteousness and of kosmic order; and as a righteous and heavenly being its food, if it have any, must be 'spiritual.'

The description continues;—

'And two of its six eyes are in the position of eyes,' *i.e.*, in the full face or Serpent-moon; 'two on the top of the head' on the Dog-moon, the Half- or New-moon; 'and two in the position of the hump,' *i.e.*, in the Unicorn-horse, the Crescent or Gibbous-moon. 'With the sharpness of these six eyes it overcomes and destroys;' [6] *i.e.*, the dread lunar face and lunar eye which, as we have seen, drives away evil and scares wicked souls. The eye is the chief power of the Ass, as it is of the Gorgô. The whole extraordinary description is, on analysis, most palpably lunar.

'Of the nine mouths three are in the head, three in the hump, and three in the inner part of the flanks.' [7] The mouths are distributed amongst the phases in the same manner as the eyes. The hump, so far as any actual animal supplies the imagery, will be that of the Indian ox. The increased number may express intensity, and the mouths be more or less Gorgonian.

'The one horn is as it were of gold and hollow. With that horn it will vanquish and dissipate all the vile corruption due to the efforts of noxious creatures.' [8] This is the pure bright unicorn's horn that drives away darkness and evil, cleanses streams and pools, and by which 'venym is defended.' [9]

'When it stales in the ocean all the sea-water will become purified. . . . If, O three-legged ass! you were not created for the water, all the water in the sea would have perished.' [10] The sea-and-water-ruling moon.

'Tîstar seizes the water more completely from the ocean with the assistance of the three-legged ass.' [11] In *Bundahis*, vii. 2, we read;—

'Every single month is the owner of one constellation; the month Tîr is the fourth month of the year, Cancer [12] the fourth constellation from Aries, so it is the owner of Cancer, into which Tîstar sprang, and displayed the characteristics of a producer of rain.' Tîstar, Tistrya or Tishtrya, is Sirius, [13] who, as the stellar protagonist, co-operates with the Moon in ruling water and regulating that humidity which is necessary to vitality.

'Tîstar was converted into three forms, the form of a man and the form of a horse and the form of a bull; thirty days and nights he was distinguished in brilliance; and in each form he produced rain ten days and nights; as the astrologers say that every constellation has three forms.' [14]

In this very interesting passage we see the Triform Moon reduplicated in a triform Sirius, himself in his glorious light a second moon. His special period of brilliance is that of the lunar course, and like the Moon, he takes the forms of horse and bull. [15]

When we get as late as the formulated systems of 'the astrologers,' each zodiacal constellation has three forms as divided into three decans, and it appears that the extra-zodiacal constellations were also regarded in some way as triform. These are the elaborations of previous simpler observation, and probably originally based upon, lunar triformity. Thus Tîstar 'the shining, majestic, the first ten nights unites himself with a body, with the body of a youth of fifteen years, a shining one, with bright eyes. The second ten nights, Tîstar unites himself with a body, proceeding along the clear space, with the body of a bull with golden hoofs. [16] The third ten nights Tîstar unites himself with a body, with the body of a horse, a shining, beautiful one, with yellow ears, with a golden housing.' [17] These phases, however, do not really apply to Sirius but to Lunus, and hence their origin.

The three-legged lunar ass is found on coins and elsewhere under the familiar form of the Triquetra, [18] the origin of which appears thus;— [19]

Fig. 1.   Fig. 2.

It is familiar on coins of Sicily as the national monetary type, a connexion however which is probably merely based upon the shape of the island—Trinacria or, as the Roman poets sometimes actually call it, Triquetra. But in the case of the Isle of Man no such reason can be admitted as explanatory. [20] Planché remarks;— 'The arms of Man are legs, or in less equivocal language, the ancient kingdom of Man was, and the island itself is still, represented in heraldry by three legs in armour, conjoined at the thighs. Our example of this heraldic curiosity [21] is particularly interesting, because the armour in which the legs are encased is the banded mail of the thirteenth century, and therefore presents us with the earliest appearance of the armorial coat of that Island and Sovereignty, after it had ceased to be Norwegian, A.D. 1264. *The origin of the bearing has yet to be discovered.'* [22] Behold it.

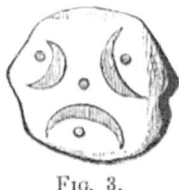

Fig. 3.

On coins of the ancient Greek city of Metabon (Metapontion-Metapontum) on the Tarentine Gulf, the three crescent legs appear in a variant phase thus;—The dots show that the three crescents are really identical with the central dot or full-moon. A favourite type on coins of Metabon is the Ear-of-corn which is always, and doubtless justly, connected with local fertility and the cult of Damater-Ceres; but at the same time the resemblance between the Ear and the Sacred Tree of the Euphrates Valley is very striking. Another coin of Metabon shows a bull's head, a type which may be lunar. [23]

A triquetric ornament appears also at Troy and Mykênê. [24]

Footnotes

1   'Using that term to denote the language of Persia during the Sassanian dynasty, A.D. 226-641' (R. B. Jr., *R.Z.*, sec. v.).

2   'Kosmogony.'

3   *O et A*, 148 *et seq.*

4   *Bundahis*, cap. xix. sec. 1. Apud E. W. West, *Pahlavi Texts*.

5   Vide *G.D.M.* i. 65.

6   Bundahis, xix. 2.

7   *Bundahis*, sec. 3.

8   *Ibid.* secs. 6, 7.

9   Vide sec. l.

10 *Bundahis*, xix. 10.

11 *Ibid.* sec. 11.

12 Kalakang-Karkinos. In another Monograph (to appear in the *Archaeologia*) I have considered the origin of the Signs of the Zodiac, and their antezodiacal character.

13 Le génie de l'étoile Sirius' (Lenormant, *Les Origines*, 31). Cf. Plutarch: Ὡρομάζης τὸν οὐρανὸν ἄτροις ἐκόσμησεν· ἕνα δ᾽ ἀστέρα πρὸ πάντων οἷον φύλακα καὶ προόπτην ἐγκατέωτησε—τὸν Σείριον (*Peri Is*. xlvii. It is now usual to deny that Plutarch wrote this Tractate; but I see no sufficient reason for the scepticism).

14 *Bundahis*, vii. 4.

15 The bovine moon is, of course, not the subject of this Monograph.

16 Cf. the golden horn of the three-legged ass: the ancient Egyptians called silver 'white-gold.'

17 *Khordah-Avesta*, xxiv. 6, ap. Spiegel and Bleeck.

18 Vide sec. III. No. XXII.

19 Vide *G.D.M.* i. 408.

20 The Rev. Is. Taylor observes, 'Mona and the Isle of Man are *perhaps* from the Welsh *mon*, separate' (*Words and Places*, 230, note 2). 'Separate' is but a feeble name to give to an island, considering also the wonderful suitability of nearly all truly archaic names. Far more probably is Man the Moon Island. The Triquetra seems to make this view almost an absolute certainty.

21 Vide Arms of Man tem. Edward I. *Mis. Cur. Coll. of Arms*. There is not the slightest evidence that the device was originally a Norman importation, or that it is really connected with any local features.

22 *The Pursuivant of Arms*, 143-4.

23 Astartê appears at times on coins as cow-headed or bull-headed, in accordance with the statement that 'she placed the head of a bull on her own head in token of sovereignty' (Sanch. i. 7). Pausanias (VI. xxiv. 5) mentions a statue of the Moon which had horns on its head, and Taurokerôs is an Orphik epithet of Selênê. So Porphyry states that the priestesses of Demeter 'called the moon, who presides over generation, a bull,' and adds, 'and Taurus is the exaltation of the Moon' (*Peri tou en Odysseia tôn Nymphôn antrou*, viii.). According to Olympiodoros (MS. *Comment.* on the *Gorgias*), 'the ancient theologists' said that 'the Moon is drawn by two bulls; by two, on account of her increase and

diminution; by bulls, because as these till the ground [Not much tillage is done by bulls], so the Moon governs all those parts which surround the earth.'

24 Vide Schliemann, *Mycenae*, figs. 382, 428, 501, 511, etc.

X
Aspects of the Moon

LIGHT BEING PLEASANT to man and Darkness more or less awful, the original aspect of the Moon is a friendly and favourable one as the head of nocturnal kosmic order, the beneficent Unicorn, the 'Righteous' Ass of the *Bundahis*, who is hated and warred against by the powers of evil. But the Moon may be the friend as well as the enemy of Night, and as such becomes Gorgonian and terrific, connected with witchcraft, evil demons, 'wicked apparitions,'[1] and all the power and horror of great darkness; whilst its changing form admits of monstrous concrete representation in art and fancy.

With reference to the Sun; the Moon may with almost equal propriety appear as the sire, mother, brother, sister, husband, bride or nurse of the mighty star; friendly to the Sun, as Inô or Sin; hostile as the Unicorn; pursued by or pursuing the Sun.

When civilization progresses sufficiently to possess a Calendar, the Moon, as time-measurer, lends invaluable assistance, and marks the months.

As lord of moisture and humidity, the Moon is connected with growth and the nurturing power of the peaceful night.

The Moon too, like the Sun, speaks of a future life, so that even the rude Congo Negro claps his hands and cries, 'So may I renew my life as thou art renewed;' [2] and in the famous Namaqua-myth 'the Moon once sent the Hare to Men to give this message, "Like as I die and rise to life again, so you also shall die and rise to life again."' [3]

According to the anthropomorphic principle the Moon appears in male or female form, and is symbolically connected with the Bull or Cow, Unicorn or Horse, Serpent, Dog and Cat, with the latter animal probably on account of phenomena of periodicity, cats' eyes shining in the dark, etc. [4] It is also at times a pearl or a good fairy. [5]

Regarded as a locality, it often appears as the abode of departed souls. So in the Kamic *Book of the Respirations*, which is probably of the epoch of the Ptolemies, the wish is expressed respecting the deceased,

'That his soul may rise to heaven in the disk of the Moon.' [6]

Such are some of the principal mythological lunar aspects. If the savage at times regards her as cleft in sunder by the angry sun, the poet at times also has his mere fancies—fancies as distinguished from the ordinary growths of mythology—and compares her to a lunatic and dying lady, tottering forth

'Led by the insane
And feeble wanderings of her fading brain.' [7]

But in health we do not speak thus, and so to this same great singer in a nobler moment she is an orbed maiden with white fire [white gold] laden.'

More grandly did Milton see her, in his stately vision, throwing 'her silver mantle o'er the dark,' even as Homer and Tennyson saw

'The stars about the moon
Look beautiful, when all the winds are laid,
And every height comes out, and jutting peak
And valley, and the immeasurable heavens
Break open to their highest.'

I append two Figures [8] illustrating the origin of the terms Caput and Cauda Draconis as applied to the moon's nodes (knots), or the two points in the heavens where the moon's orbit intersects the plane of the ecliptic.

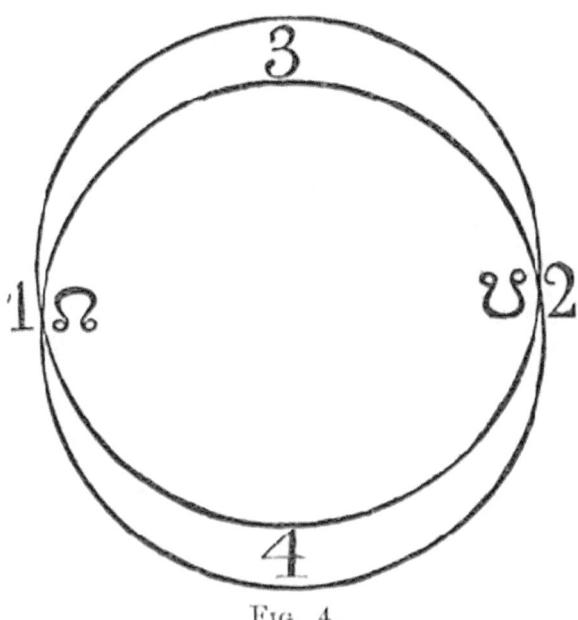

Fig. 4.

FIG. 5.

The circling path of the sun becomes similarly the Time-serpent, Kampê ('Caterpillar'), a monster slain by the solar Dionysos. [9] These two lunar serpents, twin crescents, the increasing and decreasing moon, and whose combination makes the full moon, are the two bulls which draw the moon-car on its path through space. [10]

Footnotes

1 *Akkadian Hymn* (*W.A.I.* iv. 17).

2 Tylor, P.C. ii. 272.

3 *Ibid.* i. 320.

4 Vide Dr. Hyde Clarke, *On the Relations between Pasht, the Moon, and the Cat, in Egypt*, in *T.S.B.A.* vi. 316 *et seq.*

5 Vide Gubernatis, *Zoological Mythology*, i. 54, 56.

6 Ap. M. de Horrack (*R.P.* iv. 121). On this subject vide Plutarch, *De Facie in Orbe Lunae;* Tylor, *P.C.* ii. 64; R. B. Jr., *The Archaic Solar Cult, of Egypt*, 37.

7 Shelley, *The Waning Moon.*

8 Vide Maurice, *Indian Antiquities*, ii. 201.

9 Apollod. I. ii. 2; Diod. iii. 72.

10 Vide P. 68, Note 1.

XI
The contest between the Lion and the Leopard

ERE NOTICING the final defeat of the nocturnal Unicorn, let us examine a very remarkable and most interesting instance of the triumph of Night over Day. The solar Dionysos, [1] Bakchos-Melqarth, [2] as radiate is styled Kerasphoros, Taurokerôs, and the like; and in a solar aspect generally Antauges, Chrysokomes, Chrysopes, Pyropos, etc. But one of his more occult epithets is Dithyreites, 'He-of-the-two-entrances.' According to one legend the cave in which he was concealed by Zeus from his angry consort Hêrê, [3] had two entrances; [4] and this is perfectly correct, for the Cave is the Underworld. The Two Entrances are 'the eastern gate Where the great sun begins his state,' [5] and that which in Kamic mythology is called 'the Gate of the West, the region of Bliss.' [6] These two most important Gates or Pylons are in the Kamic scheme guarded by Seb, the time-marking earth-god who, lying on the surface of the earth and looking up into the vault of heaven, watches sun, moon and stars passing through his gateways, and in so doing marks solar, lunar and sidereal time. The Sun-god Uasar-Osiris, suffering, triumphant, and in this phase in immediate relation with the individual human soul which in some occult manner must follow in his steps, 'the Great Soul, has come along the noble road, making his path above,' [7] i.e., the solar track which, according to the Vedic poet, has been prepared for the Sun by the highest gods, Mitra [8] and Varuna [9] (Ouranos), and is 'free from dust;' [10] and at eventide he reaches and passes through the western gate, to reappear in due course through the eastern gate on the next morning. Such are the two Horizon-gates of Hades, the 'Unseen' Underworld.

The influence of Mythology upon Heraldry is a subject of great interest and one which yet remains for scientific treatment, and the following myth, faithfully preserved in the latter science, presents an admirable instance of the ever-recurring contest between Astrochitôn (Starry-night) and Dionysos Dithyreites. The heraldic Leopard is a beast of 'unkindly procreation and double nature, being engendered between the Lionesse and the Pardus' or male panther, and is thus 'exorbitent of Nature's general course and intendment. This mis-begotten Beast is naturally enemy to the Lyon, and finding his own defect of courage to encounter the Lyon in fair fight, he observeth when the Lyon makes his walk near to his Den, which (in policy) he hath purposely wrought spacious and wide *in the double entrance thereof*, and narrow in the midst, so as himself being much more slender than the Lyon, may easily pass. When he seeth the Lyon, he maketh towards him hastily, as if he would bid him battell in the open fields; and when he seeth the Lyon prepared to encounter him, he betaketh him to his heeles, and maketh towards his Den with all celerity, whom the Lyon eagerly pursueth with full course, dreaming of no danger by reason of the large entrance into the Den. At length through the vehemency of his swift course, he becometh so straitned in the narrow passage in the midst of the Den that he can go neither forwards nor backwards. The Lyon being thus distressed, his enemy passeth through his Den, and cometh behind him, and gnaweth him to death.' [11]

This very singular and ancient account is evidently founded on some actual fact, but certainly on no fact connected with the habits of the animals. The simple interpretation of the occult legend is that the Lion, type of the hunting, radiate, diurnal Sun, [12] speeds across heaven towards his fate and death in the Den of the Two Entrances, the nocturnal cave tenanted by the starry, spotted Leopard of night, and where the noble beast is caught whilst going down the dark passages, [13] and perishes, although only to be reborn in triumph at the eastern gate. The two animals, as protagonists of night and day, are thus naturally hostile. There is a wide entrance to the Under-world, 'facilis descensus Averni;' the darkness flies from the light, and the Vedic poet says that 'the stars slink away, like thieves' [14] from the presence of Surya, [15] even as the cowardly leopard of the myth betakes him to his heels. 'The noble Samas' [16] pursues with all 'the vehemency of his swift course,' whilst his enemy passing through the Den, appears in heaven behind the hidden Sun, whom he thus slays; and, according to a wild-beast simile, and one, moreover, applied to an ignoble beast, gnaws to death.

Another phase of this spotted Leopard is Argos Panoptes, 'the Bright All-seeing-one,' who possessed a hundred eyes, and who was appointed by the jealous Hêrê guardian of the lunar, horned Iô, the beloved of Zeus. Amongst other exploits Argos had slain in her sleep [17] the terrible, drakontic, black-eyed, maiden-serpent, Echidna, [18] 'the Strangler,' whose dark folds were wrapped around the extinguished day, but who whilst in the heavy repose of profound gloom was suddenly annihilated by the myriad bright eyes of 'Tistar-Seirios and his fellows. But Hermes, the Wind-power upon the Clouds, the breeze of morning, [19] puts out the starry eyes and thus becomes Argeiphontês, 'the-Slayer-of-Argos,' an ancient epithet familiar to Homer. On a gem, representing the myth, [20] Hermes, as in the case of Perseus the assistant of the diurnal-power, has just decapitated Argos, an act the exact equivalent of the Gorgotomy, and his body covered with spots, the starry eyes, has fallen on the ground; behind is the Peacock, the bird of Hêrê, with its spotted, starry-eyed tail. As Mr. Ruskin notes, 'We know that this interpretation is right, from a passage in which Euripides describes the shield of Hippomedon, which bore for its sign "Argus the all-seeing, covered with eyes; open towards the rising of the stars, and closed towards their setting."' [21] The starry eyes of Argos become mediaevally the eleven thousand virgins [22] who accompany S. Ursula, 'Little-bright-one,' i.e., the moon as opposed to the sun. Riksha-arktos-ursus (ursa, dim. ursula) 'in the sense of bright, has become the name of the bear, so called either from his bright eyes or from his brilliant tawny fur' suggests Prof. Max Müller. [23] Be this as it may, the root ark 'to be bright,' is the sire of a whole tribe of words which have made myths, such as Arkas, Argo, Argos, Arjunî-Argynnis, etc.; and in the story of the Arkadian nymph Kallistô, changed into a she-bear, 'we have precisely that same confusion of thought which in India converted the seven shiners [Arkshas] into seven sages [Rishis], and in the West changed them into bears. The root, in short, furnished a name for stars, bears, and poets alike.' [24] As the Moon is Ursa-Ursula, so two famous constellations are Ursa Major and Ursa Minor.

Thus in their kosmic signification Spots denote the star-spangled heaven, Polos Ouranios, and so of the fully-attired Orphik worshipper we read;—

> 'From above the head, the all-variegated skin of a wild fawn
> Thickly spotted should hang down from the right shoulder;
> A representation of the wondrously-wrought stars and of the
> vault of heaven.' [25]

Such is the nocturnal Peacock-Leopard, slayer of darkness, slain by mightier light.

Footnotes

1 In Assyrian Dian-nisi, 'Judge-of-men', the Sun-god, as in Kam, being the particular divinity appointed by divine selection to judge.

2 Vide the *G.D.M.* ii. 100, for an account of the changes in the phases of this name. My view is now accepted by Sir G. W. Cox (*Introd.* 229).

3 Sk. Svar, 'the Gleaming-heaven'.

4 Euripides, *Bakchai*, 292.

5 *L'Allegro*, 59-60.

6 Dr. Birch in Bunsen's *Egypt's Place*, v. 147.

7 *F.R.* lxxxv.

8 As to Mitra, the Iranian Mithra and Roman Mithras, the 'Friend', consubstantial with Ahuramazda-Ormazd, vide R. B. Jr., *R.Z.*, secs. xv. xvi.

9 *Rig-Veda*, I. xxiv. 8.

10 *Ibid.* I. xxxv. 11.

11 Guillim, *D.H.* 255.

12 Vide sec. XII. subsec. 1.

13 Εὐρώεντα κέλευθα (*Od.* xxiv. 10), through which Hermes Psychopompos guides ghosts.

14 *Rig-Veda*, I. l. 2.

15 Helios-Sol.

16 Heb. Shemesh.

17 Apollod. II. i. 2. So Medousa was slain in her sleep.

18 Vedic Ahi, Gk. Echis, Lat. Anguis. 'In Echidna we have the very name of the throttling snake Ahi' (Sir G. W. Cox, *M.A.N.* ii. 334). *Anger, anguish* and *anxiety* are similarly all derived from the root *agh*, nasalised form *angh*, 'to choke'.

19 Aura-Aurora.

20 Ap. Creuzer, *Symbolik*, vol. ii. pl. viii.

21 *Q.A.* i. 28.

22 Vide R. B. Jr., *G.D.M.* ii. 80, and authorities cited.

23 *L.S.L.* ii. 300.

24 Sir G. W. Cox, *M.A.N.* i. 231. Cf. 'the names Horselberg and Ercildoune. In each case we have the berg, hill or doun of the moon-goddess Ursel, or Ursula' (*Ibid.* Introd. 160, note 4).

25 *Orphik Fragments*, vii. Diodoros (i. 11), also, states that the spotted fawn-skin signified the starry-vault. Dionysos Nebridepeplos = Herakles Astrochitôn.

XII
The Lion and the Unicorn

1. The Solar Lion

THAT THE LION is a symbol of the Sun, and more particularly of the diurnal Sun, is a fact familiar to the mythologist, and one which has already been illustrated in the preceding pages; [1] but a few further instances may suitably here be added.

In the Kamic Hymn to Ra-Har-em-akhu, [2] the diurnal sun on the horizon, we read;—'Thou roarest in smiting thy foes,' [3] the terrible roaring of flame being a link between the sun and the lion, as an Akkadian Hymn-writer says of Nindara, 'Lord-of-the-darkness,' i.e., the Nocturnal-sun, 'Thou, during thy action, roarest,' [4] and as a Vedic Hymn-writer says of Agni (Ignis) that he 'roars like a lion.' [5]

In the Inscription of Daryavush I. at El-Khargeh, the oasis of Ammon in the Libyan desert, the great god Amen-Ra, the Invisible-god revealed in the Sun-god, is addressed as 'the Lion of the double lions.' These 'two lions, two brothers,' 'the two Lion-gods,' are two solar phases as diurnal and nocturnal, Har and Set, [6] Shu and Tefnut; [7] and as there is but one solar orb, so he is '*the* Lion of the double lions.'

In the *Funereal Ritual* the Osirian, or Soul seeking divine union and communion with the Sun-god, prays;—

'Let me not be surpassed by the Lion-god:
Oh, the Lion of the Sun, who lifts his arm in the hill' [8] [of heaven].

And exclaims;—

'I am the Lions. I am the Sun.
The white lion is the phallus of the Sun.' [9]

A remarkable amulet of the Helleniko-Kamic period, copied by Caylus, [10] illustrates the occult expression 'phallus of the sun,' and also shows the solar-leonine connexion. In the centre of a circle is a closed human eye, surrounded by various animals and representations all turned towards it, and placed in the following order:—On the right hand or eastern side, a cock, a serpent, and a goose; on the north, a lizard and a thunderbolt; on the west, a scorpion and a phallus; and on the south, a lion and a dog. Caylus remarks feebly that 'Superstition is infinitely varied in its details,' but makes no attempt to explain the design; and indeed the combination is elaborate and extensive, and the design inexplicable when solely regarded either on Kamic or Hellenik principles. The single central eye is closed to show that the Sun of the Underworld is indicated, and the Lion, type of the diurnal Sun, is placed in the lower part of the design to show that the flaming sun of day has sunk beneath the horizon. By the leonine sun, is his ally the raging Dog-star, Set-Sothis, Kuôn-Seirios, Sirius, the 'Scorching.' Conversely, the Lizard, emblem of the moisture and dews of night, and as such slain by the Hellenik Sun-god Apollôn Sauroktonos, [11] is placed in the north, that is in the height of the nocturnal heaven. The Thunderbolt, which comes from the sky, also appears high in heaven. To the east, his head close on the horizon-line, stands the Cock, the solar bird of day; immediately above him and due east is the Serpent-of-light, a solar creature in Kamic symbolism and the creeping dawn-gleam in Hellenik. Above the Serpent is the Goose volant, its neck stretched towards the sun and flying from east to west. It represents the Soul of the Osirian which is said to 'cackle like a goose,' [12] to fly, and to 'alight on the road of the west of the horizon,' flying towards the Sun-god Uasar-Osiris. Near the western horizon ready to seize the sinking sun is his Scorpion-daughter the Darkness. [13] The Phallus, placed below the horizon, illustrates the secret power of the sun in the renewal of the face of the world, and is winged in order to identify it with the solar orb.

According to M. Paul Pierret (whose opinion on the matter I do not dispute), the leonto-kephalic Kamic goddesses represent the power of the solar eyes. [14]

The solar Dionysos, as Pater Bromius, 'the Roarer,' sometimes appears as leonto-kephalic in Mithraic and Gnostic symbols; [15] and in the *Bakchai* of Euripides the Chorus call upon him to put forth his dreadful might and to appear as a 'flaming lion' (πυριφλέγων λέων). [16]

The river Nile was regarded as an emanation from the kosmic Sun-god Osiris, [17] and hence is called by Homer Diipetes, [18] 'Sky-fallen,' as descended from the solar Lion. Hence the usual type of leonto-kephalic fountain-pipes, an idea which does not merely depend on the Sun being in *Leo* at the time of the inundation, for the zodiacal Leo is not an archaic Kamic constellation, and still less on the alleged contemporaneous appearance of lions in the country. Mr. King mentions an Etruscan example which shows 'figures in regular Babylonian costume, worshipping before a fountain discharging itself out of a colossal lion's head into a basin, a palm tree in the midst.' [19] Fipeke is 'the name of an Etruscan lion-headed monster, with water flowing from his mouth.' [20] He is said to have been combated by Herakles, perhaps as a rival sun-god. The Lion-sun draws up the waters of the earth and sends them down again.

The Lion and Sun form the familiar national standard of Persia, and a Persian coin given by Tavernier [21] shows the sun horned and radiate rising over the back of a lion. In the later period of the solar Mithras-cult 'the superior officials were styled Lions; hence the rites themselves are often designated as *Leontica*.' [22]

The leonto-kephalic Serpent radiate is a familiar design in Gnostic and other gems which form that large division classed by Montfaucon under the heading Abraxas. Sometimes seven stars, sometimes the sun and moon are in the field. The head often has seven rays. The Lion is occasionally shown in full; one example [23] gives the eight-rayed solar star beneath him, and the crescent-moon high in heaven.

Another interesting example of the Lion-sun is shown on a gem [24] which represents the Lion, over whom is the eight-rayed solar star, swallowing headfirst a large bee. The Bee is a creature espe-cially connected with the happy and peaceful earth-life of growth and increase, and so finds a prominent place in the symbolism of the great nature-goddess Artemis-Ephesia-Polymastos, whose chief priest was. called Essên, the King-bee. [25] The bee-swallowing Lion is the raging Athamas consuming the nourishing vegetation of the earth, whose happy voice is uplifted in the 'murmuring of innumer-able bees.' [26]

The last instance of the connexion between Sun and Lion which I shall mention is the zodiacal *Leo*, the Akkadio-Assyrian Sign of the month Abu, Aramaic Ab (July-August), the Akkadian name of which is *Ab ab-gar*, 'Fire-that-makes-fire,' the period of the full sway of the burning Athamas-Tammuz. I have treated of the original con-nexion between the Sun and the Signs in a separate monograph. [27]

2. The Contest

Such, then, being the characteristics of the mythological Lion and Unicorn, they are, like the Lion and the Leopard, naturally antago-nistic; and their contest is the converse of that of these two latter animals. As the Lion, fast in the cave, is gnawed to death by the Leopard who comes round behind him, so the Unicorn when rush-ing at the Lion sticks his horn fast in a mythic Tree behind which his opponent has taken refuge, and the Lion coming round devours him whilst thus defenceless. This incident of the story, when taken in connexion with the Leopard-myth, shows that no real animal has supplied a foundation for the belief. Spencer thus gives the legend;—

> 'Like as a Lyon whose imperial powre
> A prowd rebellious unicorn defyes,
> T'avoid the rash assault and wrathful stowre
> Of his fiers foe, him to a tree applyes,
> And when him ronning in full course he spyes,
> He slips aside; the whiles that furious beast
> His precious home, sought of his enemyes,
> Strikes in the stocke, ne thence can be releast,
> But to the mighty victor yields a bounteous feast.' [28]

Malone, commenting on the passage, 'Unicorns may be betray'd with trees,' [29] quotes *Bussy D'Ambois*, 1607;—

> 'An angry unicorne in his full career
> Charge with too swift a foot a jeweller
> That watch'd him for the treasure of his brow,
> And ere he could get shelter of a tree,
> Nail him with his rich antler to the earth.'

On the passage 'Wert thou the Unicorn, pride and wrath would confound thee, and make thine own self the conquest of thy fury,' [30] Sir Thos. Hanmer quotes from Gesner, *History of Animals*, 'The Unicorn and the Lion *being enemies by nature*, as soon as the lion sees the unicorn he betakes himself to a tree: the unicorn in his fury, and with all the swiftness of his course, running at him, sticks his horn fast in the tree, and then the lion falls upon him and kills him.'

Schliemann gives a representation of a gold plate from Mykênê with a design which he says 'represents a lion chasing a stag; the fore feet of the former are in a horizontal line to show the great speed with which he is running; he has just overtaken the stag, which sinks down before him, and his jaws are wide open to devour it. The representation of the stag *which has no horns*, is clumsy and indistinct.' [31] This is not a correct description of the design; the so-called stag, half of which only is shown, has a head and neck like that of a horse, and a peculiar crest not unlike that with which the Gryphon is at times supplied. I rather think that it has also one short horn, and far from sinking down, or flying, as might be implied from Schliemann's description, it awaits the lion's charge with lowered head, and is apparently the larger animal of the two. I do not assert that the design represents the contest of Lion and Unicorn, but it certainly bears a great resemblance to this famous duel.

The myth is of course very easy to explain in the light of the foregoing considerations. The Lion-sun flies from the rising Unicorn-moon and hides behind the Tree or Grove of the Under-world; [32] the Moon pursues and, sinking in her turn, is caught in this mysterious Tree and sun-slain. So, curiously enough, we read in a Babylonian Astrological tablet, *Sin Samsa* [33] *la* [34] *yu-ci-va; na-an-dhur aryai* [35] *u akhi.* [36]

'The Moon the Sun does not face; appearance of lions and hyaenas.' [37] So, again;—'The Moon and Sun with one another are seen: king to king hostility sends.' [38] 'The Sun in the place where the Moon set is fixed.' [39] So some Families who bear the Unicorn as Arms or Crest have such mottoes as 'Tenez le droit,' 'Cassis tutissima virtus,' etc. Moonlight as involving comparative cold and frigidity, not unnaturally connects the Moon in idea with chastity.

3. The Grove of the Underworld

As the Lion is caught in the straightness of a cave, so the Unicorn is caught in a Tree; and I will first briefly notice the mythic statements respecting this Tree and its reduplication as a Grove, and secondly consider the meaning of the occult myth.

First, then, as to the Tree-myth: the Tree constantly comes before us in connexion with the Unicorn in archaic art, [40] and in addition to the foregoing instances, I may mention a very remarkable gold signet-ring found by Schliemann at Mykênê, [41] on which is shown the conventional Tree 'whose stem certainly resembles that of a palm; it has fifteen short branches on which we see no leaves, but large clusters of a small fruit, each cluster resembling a pine apple.' One savant regards it as a pine, another as a breadfruit-tree, another as a clumsy representation of a vine; but it is none of these, being merely the conventional Tree of the myth, which in art has passed as far westwards as Mykênê, and is often a palm (Euphratean type) or poplaresque (Kamic type), the two being found jointly under Phoenician Influence. The types of the Sacred Tree of Assyria are now very familiar to us from the works of Assyriologists and otherwise; in some instances divinities stand or kneel on each side of it. 'A sacred tree, an ox, a bee' [42] were special Babylonian symbols. [43] Thus a Babylonian Cylinder [44] gives 'Sacred Tree, Seated Figure on each side, and Serpent in background,' a combination which links it with the Biblical Tree of Life; [45] and an Assyrian Cylinder [46] shows 'Sacred Tree, or Grove, with attendant Cherubim.' A Kamic representation [47] gives 'the cypress [48] shades guarded by fire-breathing uraei,' the solar-serpents of good; in these secure retreats 'the bodies of the just await their ultimate revivification.' The symbolical trees are in each case trees of the country where the myth originated.

Pherekydes [49] of Syros, a writer of reputed Phoenician descent and whose works show the strongest Oriental influence, says;—'Zas [Zeus] makes a veil large and beautiful, and works on it Earth and Ogên, [50] and the palace of Ogên;' [51] and this veil which is identical with the starry peplos of Harmonia, the bride of Kadmos 'the East-erner,' i.e., the Sun, [52] whose marriage with stellar space completes kosmic order, the god hangs on a winged oak (ἡ ὑπόπτερος δρῦς) M. Maury well observes on the myth, 'C'est là évidemment une image de la voûte du firmament, souvent figurée par un voile, et auquel un arbre est donné pour support. Il y a là une conception toute semblable à celle de l'arbre Yggdrasil de la mythologie scandinave, dont les racines s'étendent jusqu'au Niflheim et dont la tige s'élève dans les cieux.' [53] At Ragnarok 'The-Twilight-of-the-gods,' the con-clusion of the present state of things, the gigantic kosmic ash-tree Yggdrasil groans, trembles, and is set on fire; but a man and wom-an Lifthrasir ('Life-raiser'), and Lif ('Life') are preserved amid the general destruction in a sacred grove called Hoddmimir's Holt, [54] which M. Darmesteter calls the 'bois Hoddmimir équivalent du frène

Yggdrasil,' [55] a statement that is correct in a certain sense but not absolutely. Hoddmimir signifies 'Circle-Mimir' or 'Sphere-Mimir,' that is to say, the physical Mimir [56] or ocean like the Midhgardh-sormr (Great-sea-serpent), encircles the earth, and when the latter is consumed Lifthrasir and Lif are safely conveyed across ocean to the far ocean-grove, which we find in Homer;—'When thou hast sailed in the ship across the stream Okeanos [Hoddmimir], where are groves of Persephoneia [the Queen of the Underworld], poplars and willows.' [57] Stesichoros, [58] B.C. 632-552, tells how Halios (Eëlios, Helios), Hyperiôn's son, *i.e.*, son of the Climbing Sun of morning, like the Vedic Yama found out the way to the happy world which is in the west; and sailed in his golden boat-cup, which he afterwards lent to his 'dedoublement' Herakles, o'er ocean to see his dear ones in the sacred laurel [59] grove; and Mr. Ruskin, following Pindar, [60] tells us that the Greeks 'had sometimes a prophet to tell them of a land "where there is sun alike by day and alike by night, where they shall need no more to trouble the earth by strength of hands for daily bread, but the ocean breezes blow around the blessed islands, and golden flowers burn on their *bright trees* for evermore."' [61] These abodes form the western Garden of the Hesperides, where are the golden solar apples of life that resemble the fruit shown on the Conventional Tree, and were guarded in the unseen world by the 'monster serpent or drag-on' of darkness which, like the Norse Nidhoggr ('Gnawing serpent') coils around the roots of the Sacred Tree. These sacred trees appear rudely marked on many of the whorls found by Dr. Schliemann on the site of Troy, [62] and the solar Dionysos as the renewer of the life and growth of the earth, is Dendrites, [63] 'Lord-of-the-Tree,' in accordance with the imagery of the Hebrew poet-prophet, 'As the days of a tree are the days of my people, and mine elect shall long enjoy the work of their hands.' [64] Palm trees grew around the sacred 'square enclosure' of Perseus at Khemi 'in the Thebaic canton;' [65] and the circumstance connects this Perseus with the Semitic and Persian East. [66] The Sacred Grove with poplaresque trees appeared in reality within the *temenos* of many Kamic temples. It is unnecessary to add further instances.

The myth is not either specially Aryan or specially Semitic, and the Tree represents the principle of life, whilst the whole Kosmos is regarded as a mighty tree; but life is constantly being renewed from sources secret and invisible to us, especially from the Underworld, which not only represents 'the fatness of the earth beneath,' but is the 'highly mysterious cavern' where the great solar-light-bringer and life-stimulator perpetually returns. Hence, in this unknown region which the living tread not and where the sources of life are treasured up, there must by analogy be a Tree (the earthly symbol of life), trees. a grove, a happy garden, a paradise, [67] 'where souls do couch on flowers,' for man ends not at death; and in this Tree the expiring Crescent-moon, caught by her horn, pales and dies before the Sun as he goeth forth in his strength. All discord is 'harmony not understood;' the apparent contest of nature is in reality but the tranquil course of nature.

> 'Aye keeping their eternal track,
> The deities of old
> Went to and fro, and there and back,
> In boats of starry gold.' [68]

The sun is established for ever, the moon is 'a faithful witness in heaven,' the dragon-darkness is trampled under the feet of light; [69] nay, the scorpion of night, subdued to peacefulness, guards the hidden sun through the hours of gloom; and man, recognising his covenant-keeping Creator, thanks God and takes courage.

For, as is the world without, so is the world within; and the storms and splendours of nature find apt parallels in the conflicts and glories of the Soul, 'greatest of things created.' [70] Individual circumstances, if either distinctly happy or the reverse, tend somewhat to confuse the mental vision; we can get but one view of a particular prospect from one place, and we can be but in one place at a time. Yet however we may bend and reel beneath the blast of circumstance, nay, may 'falter where we firmly trod,' still, to use the noble words of a living sage, 'in health the mind is presently seen again—its overarching vault bright with galaxies of immutable lights, and the warm loves and fears that swept over us as clouds, must lose their finite character and blend with God, to attain their own perfection. But we need not fear that we can lose anything by the progress of the [noble] soul. That which is so beautiful [alike in nature and in man] must be succeeded and supplanted only by what is more beautiful, and so on for ever.'

Footnotes

1   Vide sec. III. Nos. XXIII. XXV.; sec. XI.

2   Gk. Harmachis.

3   Ap. Prof. Lushington in *R.P.* viii. 134. So the Sun is said to 'give blasts of flame from his mouth' (*F.R.* cap. xvii).

4   Ap. Lenormant, *Chaldean Magic*, 170.

5   *Rig-Veda*, III. ii. 11.

6   Vide *F.R.*, cap. xvii.

7   Vide Pierret, *Le Panthéon Égyptien*, 86.

8   Cap. lxiv., one of the oldest chapters of the *Ritual*.

9   *F.R.*, cap. xvii. The expression shows the Sun regarded as the principle of life and renewal.

10 *Recueil d'Antiquités*, vol. vi. pl. xxxviii. fig. 3.

11 Similarly, as Apollôn Smintheus, he slays the Mouse (Sk. *mûsh*, Gk. and Lat. *mus, i.e.*, 'Thief') of darkness.

12 *F.R.*, cap. xvii.

13 Vide sec. III., No. XVII.

14 *Essai sur la Mythologie Égyptienne*, 1879, p. 77; vide also Grébaut, *Des deux yeux du Disque Solaire*.

15 Vide King, *The Gnostics*, 54, 101; R. B. Jr., *G.D.M.* ii. 62.

16 *Bakchai*, 1078.

17 Νεῖλου Ὀσίριδος ἀπορρόην (Plutarch, *Peri Is.* xxxviii.).

18 *Od.* iv. 477.

19 *A.G.R.* i. 168, note.

20 Prof. Sayce in Cooper's *Archaic Dict.* In voc.

21 *Travels in Persia*, i. 50.

22 King, *The Gnostics*, 59.

23 Montfaucon, vol. ii. pt, ii. pl. cxlix. fig. 1.

24 *Ibid.*, pl. cxlviii. fig. 5.

25 Vide K. O. Müller, *Doric Race*, i. 403-4.

26 Vide *G.D.M.* i. 401 *et seq.*

27 For further detail respecting the leonine sun, vide *R.P.* Knight, *Symbolical Language of Ancient Art and Mythology*, edit. 1876, pps. 75, 97, 112; R. B. Jr., *G.D.M.* ii. 61.

28 *Faerie Queene*, II. v. 10.

29 *Julius Caesar*, ii. 1.

30 *Timon of Athens*, iv. 3.

31 *M. and T.*, 308-9, Vide sec. III., No. XXXIII.

32 Vide subsec. 3.

33 Heb. שֶׁמֶשׁ

34 Heb. לֹא

35 Heb. אוֹיָרְתְ

36 Heb. צִיִּים (*Isaiah*, xiii. 21.)

37 *T.S.B.A.* iii. 305. It will be observed that Hebrew is a dialect of the Semitic Babylonio-Assyrian.

38 *W.A.I.* III. lviii., 1-2, ap. Prof. Sayce.

39 *Ibid*. III. lxiv. Rev. 22.
40 Vide Frontispiece; sec. III., Nos. I. II. III. VI. VIII. XII. XIII. XVIII. XXVII.; sec. VI.
41 *M. and T.*, fig. 530, p. 354.
42 *A.M.* iii. 32.
43 As to the Bee, vide subsec. 1.
44 Smith, *C.A.G.*, 88.
45 Vide Menant, *La Bible et les Cylindres Chaldéens*, 8.
46 *C.A.G.*, 85.
47 Cooper, *Serpent Myths of Anct. Egypt*, fig. 33, p. 19.
48 Vide Lajard, *Sur le Culte du Cyprès pyramidal*.
49 Vide p. 53.
50 Cf. Ogyges, Ogre, and the Norse Oegir, 'the Dread.'
51 Ap. Clem. Alex. *Stromata*, vi. 2.
52 Kadmos of course also represents Semitic colonisation (vide *G.D.M.*, cap. X. sec. ii., *Kadmos and Thebai*).
53 *Histoire des Religions de la Grèce Antique*, iii. 253. Vide also Lenormant, *Les Origines*, i. 568.
54 For an account and explanation of the Ragnarok-myth, vide R. B. Jr. *R.M.A.*, 35 *et seq.*
55 *O et A*, 299.
56 The mental Mimir is 'memory,' wisdom; cf. Sk. root *mi*, to measure, judge, observe; Lat. *memor*, Ang.-Sax. *meomer*.
57 *Od*. x. 508.
58 Ap. Athenaios, xi. 4.
59 I.e., 'bright' grove. 'The dawn was called δάφνη, the burning, so was the laurel as wood that burns easily' (Prof. M. Müller, *L.S.L.*, ii. 549, note. Cf. Philodaphnos as an epithet if Apollôn and Dionysos).
60 *Olymp.*, ii.
61 *Q.A.* i. 50.
62 *Troy and its Remains*, pl. xxxiv.
63 Pindar, *Frag.* cxxx.; Plout. *Peri Is.* xxxv.
64 *Isaiah*, lxv. 12.
65 Herod. ii. 91.
66 Vide sec. VII.
67 The Iranian *pairidaêza*, 'enclosure.'
68 Gerald Massey, *A Book of the Beginnings*, i. 310.
69 Vide Clermont-Ganneau, *Horus et Saint Georges*; Baring-Gould, *Curious Myths of the Middle Ages*, S. George. So in this year's Royal. Academy, apropos of Sir J. Gilbert's picture *Fair St. George*, we read; 'Smiting the dragon with his [solar] spear [of light], he was sorely wounded and thrown down. Then St. George called to the Princess [his love and bride the Dawn] to bind her girdle [cf. the *Kredemnon* of Inô, sec. VIII.] about the dragon's neck and not to be afeared. The dragon followed as it had been a meek beast and debonayre.' Day and night, light and darkness, contended no longer; kosmic order was restored, and 'the raven-down of darkness' was 'smoothed' 'till it smiled.'
70 *F.R.* lxxiii.

Abbreviations

Brown, R. Jr., *G.D.M.—The Great Dionysiak Myth*. (London: Longmans, 1877-8.)

— *R.M.A.—The Religion and Mythology of the Aryans of Northern Europe*, 1880.

— *R.Z.—The Religion of Zoroaster*, 1879.

Cox, Rev. Sir G. W., *M.A.N.—Mythology of the Aryan Nations*.

— *Introd.—Introduction to Mythology and Folklore*, 1881.

Cussans, J. E., *H.H.—The Handbook of Heraldry*.

Darmesteter, J., *O et A.—Ormazd et Ahriman*.

Dennis, G., *C.C.E.—Cities and Cemeteries of Etruria*, edit. 1878.

Fosbroke, Rev. T. D., *E.A.—Encyclopedia of Antiquities*.

Guillim, J., *D.H.—A Display of Heraldrie*, edit. 1660.

King, C. W., *A.G.R.—Antique Gems and Rings*.

Müller, Prof. M., *L.S.L.—Lectures on the Science of Language*, 6th edit.

Rawlinson, Rev. Prof., *A.M.—Ancient Monarchies*.

Ruskin, J., *Q.A.—The Queen of the Air*.

Schliemann, H., *M. & T.—Mycenae and Tiryns*.

Smith, G., *C.A.G.—Chaldean Account of Genesis*, 2nd edit.

Tylor, E. B., *P.C.—Primitive Culture*.

F.R.—The Egyptian Funereal Ritual. Translated by Dr. Birch.

R.P.—Records of the Past. (London: Bagster & Sons, 1873-81.)

T.S.B.A.—Transactions of the Society of Biblical Archaeology.

W.A.I.—Cuneiform Inscriptions of Western Asia.

INDEX

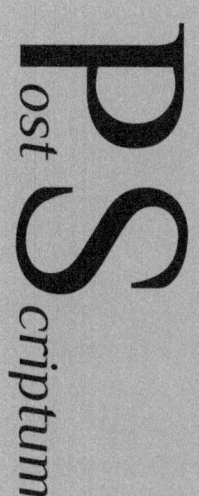

Post **S**criptum

Brown,
a vivid
Victorian …

About Robert Brown Junior

VAMzzz Publishing

Biography Brown

– A vivid Victorian mind trapped in
  Barton-on-Humber

Robert Brown Junior, FSA (Fellow of the
Society of Antiquaries), MRAS (Member
of the Royal Astronomical Society), A.M.,
(1844-1912) is often erroneously portrayed
as an English Orientalist or Assyriologist and
Egyptologist. Actually, he was an English
Solicitor in Barton-on-Humber, a small
market town, once an important centre for
the manufacture of bicycles, located along
the south bank of River Humber. He was
also a writer on archaic religion, mythology,
and pioneered in the research of ancient
Babylonian astronomy.

Robert Brown Junior was educated at
Cheltenham College, Gloucestershire,
considered one of the best public schools of
the Victorian period. His father, Robert Brown
F.R.S., Solicitor and Registrar of the County
Court, Barton-on-Humber wrote a number
of tracts on religious matters including:
Jesuitism, or, *The Devil's travesty of the Son of
the Kingdom.* He founded Brown and Son,
Solicitors, when Robert Brown Junior joined
it. Both his job and his living place Junior
perceived as boring, but he managed to escape
his daily state of affairs with a lifelong research
activity and publishing books about his fields
of interest. Thus, in his day, Brown Junior
became a popular writer.

During the 1870s and 1880s he tried to prove the influence of ancient Semitic cultures on Hellenic religious mythology. Along with George Cox and Abram Palmer, he enthusiastically embraced and promoted the school of nature mythology originated by Max Müller. At this period when solar, lunar, and stellar interpretations of mythology were being linked to India and the Rig Veda, Brown Junior argued for Semitic influences on Greek mythology. Circa 1883 Brown Junior started a research on the origin of the extra-zodiacal constellations. This resulted in 1899-1900 in the two *Volumes of Researches into the Origin of the Primitive Constellations of Greeks, Phoenicians and Babylonians,* works that are now outdated due to many new discoveries like the Mul Apin–tables and more.

For many years Brown was dependant on the guidance given to him, amongst others, by the assyriologist George Bertin (1848-1891). In the late 19th-century journal *The Academy* it is Robert Brown Junior, who George Bertin is referring to for breaching trust and publishing some of Bertin's significant work, unacknowledged, as it was Brown's own work. Trying to make out at this late stage what was Brown's own work and what was a copy of the work of others is an impossible task.

It seems that for a time Robert Brown Junior practiced fraudulent physical mediumship ▶

'Along with George Cox and Abram Palmer, Brown Jr. enthusiastically embraced and promoted the school of nature mythology originated by Max Müller.'

3

▶   (around 1889-1891), and his "séances", generally resulting in a table levitation trick, were investigated by officers of *The Society for Psychical Research.* His wife Ann was connected with the Society for Psychical Research in London. In his book *Demonology and Witchcraft* (1889) a Robert Brown (not Robert Brown Junior) mentions a lecture and demonstration of mesmerism being held in the Temperance Hall in Barton-on-Humber in 1889. Brown Junior was also considered to be the author of the privately printed humorous pamphlet/monograph titled *Totemism* (1887), described as an admirable burlesque upon the current scientific absurdities on the study of totemism.

The writer was frequently mistaken for other individuals with the name Robert Brown. In his presidential address for 1896, the prominent folklorist Edward Clodd erroneously mentioned the death of Robert Brown in 1895. Robert Brown Junior died at the age of 68 years in 1912. Brown very much felt his isolation in Barton-on-Humber - and his distance from London to attend meetings. Eventually he became the only member of his family to remain living in Barton-on-Humber. He wrote the well received history, *Notes on the Earlier History of Barton-on-Humber* (2 Volumes, 1906-1908). Nevertheless, his endorsement of a number of vernacular words as specimens of the Danish past of Barton-on-Humber was considered erroneous. ■

Other publications:

- *Poseidôn: a Link between Semite, Hamite, and Aryan (1872)*
- *The Great Dionysiak Myth (2 Volumes, 1877-1878) A third volume was contemplated but never published.*
- *The Religion of Zoroaster, Considered in Connection with Archaic Monotheism (1879)*
- *The Religion and Mythology of the Aryans of Northern Europe (1880)*
- *Language, and Theories of its Origin (1881)*
- *The Unicorn – A Mythological Investigation (1881)*
- *The Law of Kosmic Order (1882)*
- *Eridanus: River and Constellation. A Study of the Archaic Southern Asterisms (1883)*
- *The Myth of Kirke (1883)*
- *The Phainomena, or, 'Heavenly Display' of Aratos: Done into English Verse (1885)*
- *Semitic Influence in Hellenic Mythology (1898)*
- *Researches into the Origin of the Primitive Constellations of the Greeks, Phoenicians, and Babylonians (2 Volumes, 1899-1900)*
- *Notes on the Earlier History of Barton-on-Humber (2 Volumes, 1906-1908)*

'For many years Brown was dependant on the guidance given to him, amongst others, by the assyriologist George Bertin.'

VAMzzz Publishing

Paper books

VAMzzz Publishing is located in the very centre of old Amsterdam, in The Netherlands. Our publishing company creates high quality revised editions of five star occult, witchcraft, Gothic and esoteric classics, mostly written in the Fin de siècle-period and early 20th century.

As a publisher, we deeply respect the writer of any book we choose, so we join our forces (top level graphic design & thirty years of occult studies) to produce enchanting volumes which maximize the reading pleasure and inform, often with extra added information. In contrast to the current trend of digital screen addiction, we think, this variety of literature needs to be presented on paper. *No e-books, but real books!*

Apart from republications of valuable but forgotten books, we are also in the preparation of new publications on topics such as self-healing, magic, new astrology and more.

Previews of all books including a complete table of contents can be viewed on www.vamzzz.com. More books will be added to the list. *VAMzzz Publishing* strives to publish new volumes every month. Please visit our website regularly for the latest updates.

VAMzzz Publishing
P.O. Box 3340
1001 AC Amsterdam
The Netherlands
contactvamzzz@gmail.com
www.vamzzz.com

Recommended

Amazons
- Two publications in one -

I. The Amazons by
Guy Cadogan Rothery

*II. Religious Cults
Associated With the
Amazons* by
Florence Mary Bennett

104 pages, Paperback
ISBN 978-94-92355-08-9

The Amazons (1910) by Guy Cadogan Rothery (1863-1940) and *Religious Cults Associated with the Amazons* (1912) by Prof. Florence Mary Bennett (1880–1954) are still two of the very few books ever published on these legendary female warriors. The world of the Amazons lies scattered between legend and historical fact. The Athenians in particular were most insistent about the historical reality of a nation consisting only of women warriors. The Amazons, whether legendary or real, were not confined to the Balkan-Black Sea regions bordering to ancient Greece. As Guy Cadogan Rothery points out, they were known on four different continents. Florence Mary Bennett examines the traditional Amazons, as mentioned in Greek sources, and relates them to several goddess cults of ancient Greece and Asia Minor. Among them the cult of the Great Mother, the Ephesian Artemis, Artemis Astrateia and Aphrodite. Bennet deals with historical facts in an outstanding piece of scholarly research, unveiling not just many historical data about this ancient warrior tribe, but also providing surprising insights into the image evolution of Greek Gods, the double axe symbol and more.

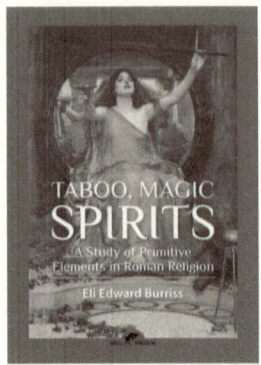

Taboo, Magic, Spirits
A study of primitive elements in Roman religion
by Eli Edward Burriss
200 pages, Paperback, ISBN 9789492355034

In Ancient Rome Mana was the term used for a mysterious, magical medium, which could be helpful or harmful (Taboo). Just like the Chinese qi, it could empower the positive and the negative. Contents: Mana, Magic and Animism – Positive and Negative Mana (Taboo) – Miscellaneous Taboos – Magic Acts: The General Principles – Removing Evils by - Magic Acts – Incantation and Prayer– Naturalism and Animism.

Chaldean Magic
It's Origin and Development
by François Lenormant
454 pages, Paperback, ISBN 9789492355027

The essentials of magic in Chaldea are presented inside a context of comparison or contrast to Egyptian, Median, Turanian, Finno-Tartarian and Akkadian magic, mythologies, religion and speech. Interesting is the Chaldean demonology, with its incubus, succubus, vampire, nightmare and many Elemental spirits, most of them coalesced with the primal powers of nature.

Ophiolatreia
Rites and Mysteries of Serpent Worship
Author: Hargrave Jennings
186 pages, Paperback, ISBN 9789492355126

An account of the rites and mysteries connected with the origin, rise and development of serpent worship in various parts of the world, enriched with interesting traditions, and a full description of the celebrated serpent mounds & temples, the whole forming an exposition of one of the phases of phallic, or sex worship.

Là-Bas
A Journey into the Self
by Joris-Karl Huysmans
378 pages, Paperback, ISBN 9789492355058

The plot of *Là-Bas* concerns the novelist Durtal, who is disgusted by the emptiness and vulgarity of the modern world. He seeks relief by turning to the study of the Middle Ages. Through his contacts in Paris, Durtal discovers that Satanism is not a thing of the past but alive and kicking in turn of the century France. The novel culminates with a description of a black mass.

Devil-worship in France
Or The Question of Lucifer
by Arthur Edward Waite
240 pages, Paperback, ISBN 9789492355065

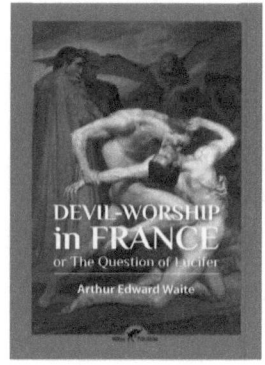

In *Devil-Worship in France,* Waite attempts to discern what is genuine from what is fake in the evidence of 19th century Satanism. To get the answers he spends a great deal of time investigating the French Masonic echelon, debunking a "conspiracy of falsehood" and determining what should be understood by Satanism and what not. Huysmans' diabolical novel *Là-Bas* (1891) inspired Waite to write this sceptical analysis.

Voodoos and Obeahs
Phases of West India Witchcraft
by Joseph J. Williams
374 pages, Paperback, ISBN 9789492355119

This work goes into great depth concerning the New World-African connection and is highly recommended if you want a deep understanding of the dramatic historical background of Haitian and Jamaican magic and witchcraft, and the profound influence of imperialism, slavery and racism on its development. Williams includes numerous quotations from rare documents and books on the topic.

Fairy Mythology (Volume 1)
Romance and Superstition of Various Countries 1
by Thomas Keightley
404 pages, Paperback, ISBN 9789492355096

Fairy Mythology (Volume 2)
Romance and Superstition of Various Countries 2
by Thomas Keightley
404 pages, Paperback, ISBN 9789492355102

The term Fairy covers all kinds of nature spirits, not just the tiny sugar sweet creatures hovering around flowers. A unique and impressive book on this subject, published in a revised 2 volume-edition. No wiccan or pagan can afford to leave these books unopened. About Elves, Dwarfs, Kobolds, Trolls, Changelings, Meremaids, Nisses, Fairies, Brownies, Puck and other Elemental spirits all over the world.

Etruscan Magic & Occult Remedies
(Two volumes in one book)
Charles Godfrey Leland
628 pages, Paperback, ISBN 9789492355003

Part One of the book offers complete and detailed insight in the Etruscan and Roman rooted pantheon of the Tuscan Streghe (witches). Part Two describes many of their spells, incantations, sorcery and several lost divination methods. Much information in this book, Leland received first hand from the Tuscan witches Maddalena and Marietta.

Testament of Solomon
A First Century AD Grimoire
76 pages, Paperback, ISBN 9789492355041

A first century AD grimoire, and therefore the oldest, and least known, of all grimoires (magical instruction books) in the occult tradition. The book describes health inflicting demons of zodiacal decans, summoned by King Solomon, and how he controlled them to use their forces to build his temple and more. Translated by F. C. Conybeare, appeared first in the *Jewish Quarterly Review* of October, 1898.

Aradia
Gospel of the Witches
by Charles Godfrey Leland
174 pages, Paperback, ISBN 9789492355010

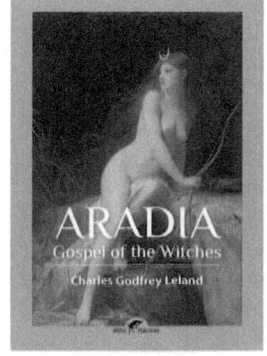

This wonderful book describes the creation according to Italian witch-lore. We also read about the witch-meeting or sabbath (treguenda) and the book contains many original magical recipes, like spells for love and good fortune. Diana is further connected to the Moon and the fairy world.